TOP SECRET FILES

GANGSTERS AND BOOTLEGGERS

TOP SECRET FILES

GANGSTERS AND BOOTLEGGERS

STEPHANIE BEARCE

PRUFROCK PRESS INC.
WACO, TEXAS

Library of Congress Cataloging-in-Publication Data

Bearce, Stephanie, author.
Top secret files : gangsters and bootleggers / by Stephanie Bearce.
   1 online resource.
Includes bibliographical references.
Description based on print version record and CIP data provided by publisher; resource not viewed.
ISBN 978-1-61821-461-4—pbk.
ISBN 978-1-61821-460-7—pdf
ISBN 978-1-61821-511-6—ePub
1. Prohibition--United States--History--Juvenile literature. 2. Criminals--United States--History--20th century--Juvenile literature. 3.   United States--History--1919-1933--Juvenile literature. 4.   United States--Social life and customs--1918-1945--Juvenile literature. I. Title.
HV5089
364.106'6092273--dc23
                                    2015031268

Image credits: Page 86: Property of Museum of History & Industry, Seattle • Page 88: Property of Museum of History & Industry, Seattle

Edited by Lacy Compton

Cover design by Raquel Trevino and layout design by Allegra Denbo

ISBN-13: 978-1-61821-461-4

Printed in the United States of America.

At the time of this book's publication, all facts and figures cited are the most current available. All telephone numbers, addresses, and website URLs are accurate and active. All publications, organizations, websites, and other resources exist as described in the book, and all have been verified. The author and Prufrock Press Inc. make no warranty or guarantee concerning the information and materials given out by organizations or content found at websites, and we are not responsible for any changes that occur after this book's publication. If you find an error, please contact Prufrock Press Inc.

Prufrock Press Inc.
P.O. Box 8813
Waco, TX 76714-8813
Phone: (800) 998-2208
Fax: (800) 240-0333
http://www.prufrock.com

TABLE OF CONTENTS

PROHIBITION PAIN

SECRETS AND SCANDALS

SHOOTOUTS AND SCOUNDRELS

MOST WANTED

WARNING!

HEY YOU DARBS AND DOLLS! BE WARNED! THE STORIES IN THIS BOOK ARE SOME HUMDINGERS AND THEY MIGHT JUST GIVE YOU THE HEEBIE-JEEBIES. THERE'S SOME NASTY STUFF ABOUT PEOPLE GETTING "BUMPED OFF" AND "BEING TAKEN FOR A RIDE." IF YOU THINK THERE'S A CHANCE YOU MIGHT UPCHUCK OR HAVE A KITTEN WHEN YOU READ ABOUT BLOOD AND GUTS, THEN YOU NEED TO GET A WIGGLE ON AND SKIP THIS JOINT.

BUT IF YOU'RE KEEN ON LEARNING THE TRUTH, THEN JEEPERS-CREEPERS, KEEP ON READING!

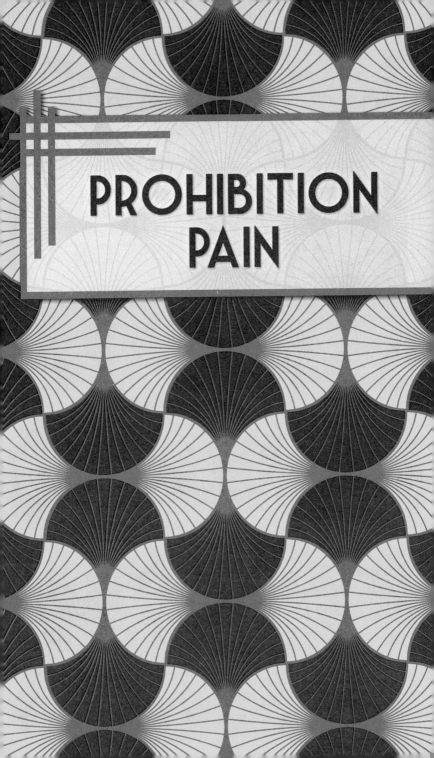

PROHIBITION
PAIN

CARRIE NATION

WOMAN WITH A MISSION

Carrie Nation holding a hatchet

Wichita saloon in Kansas destroyed by Carrie Nation, 1901

Men were laughing and joking at the bar and a few cowboys were playing a friendly game of poker, when the door to the saloon burst open and in walked a huge woman carrying a hatchet.

"Men, I have come to save you from a drunkard's fate!" the woman shouted.

Then she ran to the bar and began smashing bottles of whiskey and kegs of beer. She slammed her hatchet against the saloon mirror and shards of glass flew through the air. Men ducked under tables and ran for the door. The woman kept swinging the hatchet—smashing tables, breaking windows, and destroying everything in the bar.

Outside the saloon, a small group of women cheered her on by singing hymns and chanting, "Save yourself from demon rum!" A couple of the women were armed with large rocks. They heaved the stones through the windows and glass sprayed through the air. Townspeople ran through the streets shouting, "Carrie Nation is here!"

Within a few minutes, a crowd gathered around the saloon. Some people were cheering for Carrie Nation and her saloon busters, while others yelled at her to "get out of town." The sheriff and his deputy arrived to a scene of chaos. Men cut and bleeding, smashed glass and furniture, the stench of spilled whiskey and beer, and the sound of women singing church hymns.

The sheriff strode into the saloon and ordered Carrie Nation to stop. The hatchet smashed another table.

"I'm on a mission from God," Nation said.

And she went on smashing and wrecking the room. It took both the sheriff and his deputy to get the hatchet away from Nation. She was 6 feet tall, weighed 175 pounds, and was well-muscled from years of hard physical labor. With the help of a few more men, Carrie Nation and her followers were arrested and marched off to the city jail.

But Carrie Nation didn't mind. She had her victory. One more saloon was out of commission and another night in jail didn't bother her. She'd spent so many nights in jails that she couldn't count them all. It was all

Nation in the Wichita jail, 1901

worth it if she could save the United States from the evils of drinking alcohol. One day, her country would thank her.

Carrie Nation was one of the leaders of the Temperance Movement. These were people who believed that banning the sale and consumption of alcohol would improve life in America. They explained that drunken fathers abused their children and wives, and that drinking alcohol led to corruption and law breaking. Many people agreed. They just had to look in the jails to see people who had been arrested for breaking laws while they were drunk. The people who wanted alcohol outlawed were called the "Drys."

The "Wets" were people who wanted alcohol to remain legal. They believed that it was up to each individual to make the decision about whether or not to consume alcohol and how much to drink. The Wets did not believe that people would stop drinking alcohol just because it was outlawed. They thought that people would still find a way to get alcohol and it would probably be through the black market or illegal dealers. The Wets warned that banning alcohol would lead to more crime.

The fight went on for years. Carrie Nation conducted her first saloon attack in Kiowa, KS, in June of 1900. She led groups of women in smashing saloons for nearly 10 years and was arrested more than 30 times. In a time when women were not allowed to vote, Nation believed the only way she could get her point across was to demonstrate in public.

Other people in the Temperance Movement were not as destructive as Carrie Nation. Many men and women stood outside saloons across America and lectured the patrons about the evils of alcohol. Some preachers went into the bars and tried to give sermons to the customers, but they were usually ignored and sometimes chased out of the building. They might have gotten pelted with food or had drinks thrown in their face. The Drys considered it a war against alcohol and the Wets felt it was a war against their freedom of choice.

Carrie Nation conducted her first saloon attack in Kiowa, KS, in June of 1900. She led groups of women in smashing saloons for nearly 10 years and was arrested more than 30 times.

When America entered World War I in 1917, President Woodrow Wilson ordered a temporary wartime prohibition on alcohol in order to save the grain for producing food. The people of the Temperance Movement pushed even harder for this temporary prohibition to be made permanent. In 1919, the 19th amendment was ratified and the manufacture, transportation, and sale of intoxicating liquors were banned in the United States.

The American Issue, January 25, 1919

Carrie Nation didn't live to see Prohibition in America. She died in 1911, but many of her followers celebrated the day by smashing kegs of beer and cases of liquor in the streets. They were sure that this would be a new era in America where crime would decrease, jail cells would be empty, and society would benefit from being sober.

During the first few months of Prohibition, the police did report a drop in the number of arrests for drunkenness, and there was a 30% drop in the amount of alcohol consumed. But many people still wanted to drink alcohol. Men had just returned from fighting in the Great War and wanted to cut loose and celebrate. Women had just received the right to vote with the passage of the 18th Amendment. They wanted to test out their new freedoms. The public was determined to figure out ways to keep the whiskey flowing.

Bootlegging (making and selling illegal liquor) became the new crime that the police had to fight. People built their own stills and began producing and selling illegal whiskey, moonshine, and liquors. Clubs opened up where people could gather to drink the illegal alcohol and gangsters began transporting and selling the goods. And instead of reducing the number of saloons, it actually increased them. In 1927, there were 30,000 speakeasies (illegal bars) in New York City. That was twice as many saloons as there were before Prohibition.

For 13 years, Carrie Nation's Temperance Movement ruled America, but in 1933, President Franklin Delano Roosevelt signed the 21st Amendment that repealed the prohibition of alcohol. And this time, it was the bootleggers who were out of a job.

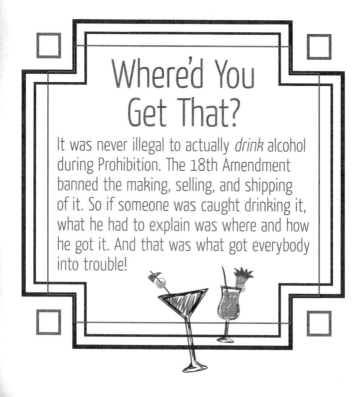

Where'd You Get That?

It was never illegal to actually *drink* alcohol during Prohibition. The 18th Amendment banned the making, selling, and shipping of it. So if someone was caught drinking it, what he had to explain was where and how he got it. And that was what got everybody into trouble!

NYPD pours liquor into sewer following raid, 1921

BYE-BYE BOOZE, HELLO BOOTLEGGERS

A bootlegger transports alcohol

The mourners lifted the casket on to their shoulders and marched through the streets of Broadway. Dressed in dark suits and black dresses, there was no crying or sobbing, just glasses of champagne and wine lifted high in a final farewell to King Alcohol. It was the night before Prohibition, January 17, 1920, and people across America were either mourning the end of alcohol or celebrating the beginning of a dry country.

Restaurants and hotels in New York held many funeral-themed parties. Tables were draped with black cloth, caskets held black bottles, and guests ate black caviar. The Café de Paris held a Cinderella-themed ball, and at midnight, all of

the liquor disappeared. Partygoers at the Hotel Vanderbilt polished off 100 cases of champagne as they said good-bye to alcohol.

The members of the Temperance Movement and the Dry voters celebrated with church services that welcomed in a new age of sobriety. Famous preacher Billy Sunday declared America a better and safer place now that the production of alcohol was illegal. Thousands of people were sure that he was right and a new era of peace had arrived in America.

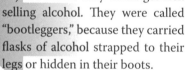

Some men sewed vests with special pockets that they filled with flasks of alcohol and then simply put a coat over the top.

But there were some people who saw Prohibition as an opportunity to make some fast cash. They knew many Americans still wanted to drink wine, beer, and alcohol. They were willing to bring in alcohol from Canada and Mexico and sell it illegally. They believed it was worth the risk of being caught and sent to jail because they could get rich

selling alcohol. They were called "bootleggers," because they carried flasks of alcohol strapped to their legs or hidden in their boots.

They soon learned that the demand for alcohol was so great that they needed to figure out ways to transport mass quantities of liquor. Some men sewed vests with special pockets that they filled with flasks of alcohol and then simply put a coat over the top. Others made false compartments in their cars or trucks. Some bootleggers hid the alcohol in coffins, others inside hearses. The bootleggers correctly believed that the police didn't want to disturb a dead body and wouldn't do a search.

Some bootleggers even tried transporting liquor in hollowed-out eggs. Others pumped alcohol into watermelons and what looked like innocent fruit was actually illegal liquor storage.

The Drys had underestimated Americans' desire for alcohol. The start of Prohibition did not mean the end of wine and beer—it meant that the manufacture of alcohol moved from legal breweries, wineries, and distilleries to smuggling and production by gangsters and bootleggers. It also brought in a wave of crime like America had never seen before.

The Birth of Moonshine

Moonshine was a term used for illegal homemade alcohol. The original term *moonshine* was used by British settlers to describe any job that had to be done at night. Bootleggers started calling their illegal alcohol moonshine because they were less likely to get caught if they made it and moved it at night.

Revenuers carrying packages of confiscated liquor, 1921

W. A. Green, Chief Prohibition Inspector, 1925

THE REVENUERS ARE COMING!

The still was well hidden, placed deep in the woods and camouflaged by tree branches and boulders. Two men were busy filling jugs from the spout of the still. One man stood as lookout, his shotgun at the ready. They were all alert for the sound of snapping branches, the skittle of rocks, or any other noise that would warn them that someone was coming their way.

> They knew the revenuers had been in their county. A friend's still had been smashed and he had been hauled off to jail.

He had to pay bail money to get out and bribe money to the judge. It was costly to get caught. Even worse, rumor was that the revenuers were carrying guns and were ready and willing to shoot it out. It made a bootlegger kind of nervous.

Largest confiscated still, 1922

Confiscated whiskey, 1921

Throughout rural America, scenes like this played out on a weekly basis. With the start of Prohibition, the department of the Internal Revenue Service was put in charge of enforcing the new anti-alcohol laws. Some of the officers took their job seriously and were vigilant in seeking out the stills of moonshiners and the cargo of rum-runners. But other officers really didn't think the law was fair. They didn't believe the government had the right to decide if a person could make alcohol or not. It had been legal for centuries and was still legal in other countries all over the world. The officers themselves had made their own wine or beer; it was a common custom of the day. These officers looked the other way or just didn't work too hard to find the stills.

Other officers saw the vast sums of money the bootleggers were making selling the alcohol and decided they wanted a cut. These officers flagrantly broke the law by taking bribes from bootleggers and gave the gangsters warnings so they could avoid the raids.

Part of the problem was that there were far more people making and selling illegal alcohol than there were revenue officers. There were 1,550 federal agents hired, but they had to watch more than 18,700 miles of coastline. It was next to impossible for them to stop all of the alcohol that was made and brought into the country.

And to make it even more difficult, the laws of Prohibition never actually made it illegal to *drink* alcohol. It was perfectly legal for people to own and consume alcohol in their homes. Many wealthy people stocked up before Prohibition was signed into law. They kept barrels of wine and kegs of beer in their cellars and had bottles of whiskey and rum stored in their basements.

It also was legal for wine to be used for religious purposes, so many men declared themselves rabbis so they could legally purchase sacramental wines. And doctors could prescribe alcohol for medicinal purposes. There were lots of prescriptions written during Prohibition! Coughs, colds, hay fever, sprained fingers—it could all be helped with a prescription for alcohol.

Patent medicine became very popular during Prohibition. Peruna Tonic was a famous "Prohibition tonic," and it contained 18% alcohol. A few gulps of Peruna, and the patient would be just as drunk as if he had been drinking wine or beer, but Peruna was legal to buy from the drugstore.

It made the Revenuers' job almost impossible. But it was a job that had to be done according the new constitutional amendment, even if half of America was against it.

GET THE GOODS

Prohibition
Word Scramble

See if you can unscramble these Prohibition words:

Pnioithbrio

ilaegll

rriCae ntNoia

mionnheos

ryDs

aetsgn

Wste

emwnal

sgtrogboeel

udkrn

eeunesrrv

netpaecrme

iqloru

hatthec

onaosl

Answer Key:
Prohibition, Carrie Nation, Drys, Wets, bootleggers, revenuers, liquor, saloon, illegal, moonshine, agents, lawmen, drunk, temperance, hatchet

BOOTLEGGER MAZE

DIRECTIONS: SEE IF YOU CAN MAKE IT ALL THE WAY THROUGH THE BOOTLEGGERS MAZE

START

POLICE

TEMPERANCE

SPEAKEASY

FINISH

SECRETS & SCANDALS

SPEAKEASIES

It looked like a regular grocery shop. There were tins of crackers, cans of meat, displays of vegetables, and a cooler full of soda pop. Visitors to the store came through the front of the shop, just like regular grocery store customers, and they might even purchase a can of soup or pork and beans, but their real mission was at the back of the store. There, people who had been told what to look for could spot a hidden door. When they knocked on the door, they had to whisper a secret code.

Speakeasy doorslot

Speakeasy secret knock

Inside the door, there were steps that led down to another door. Another set of code words had to be given. The last door opened into a room crowded with small tables and chairs and filled with the smoke of cigarettes. Men in suits and neckties sat talking to young women with short hair and scandalous beaded dresses that showed their ankles. The smell of whiskey mixed with the scent of cigarettes. Most of the people were sipping drinks and everyone was laughing and chatting. The noise only died down when there was a singer on the stage.

It was a speakeasy—an illegal liquor club that became popular during Prohibition. They got their name because patrons had to speak quietly—or easy—about the location and the passwords. Because they were selling liquor, the speakeasies were targets for police raids and patrons could be arrested for engaging in the illegal trade of alcohol.

But despite the risk, thousands of people went to the speakeasies. Saloons had been outlawed by Prohibition. The police ordered all of the local bars to be closed. But that didn't stop people from wanting a place to gather and drink. The former saloonkeepers opened up secret bars, and so did lots of other people. Bootleggers and moonshiners expanded their business and put bars in basements, hid them in attics or old stores, and even put them underground in caves and mines. Any place that was away from the prying eyes of the police was a possible home for a speakeasy.

Before Prohibition, women were not allowed in saloons and most American women did not drink hard liquor. They may have had a little wine, but they didn't drink whiskey, rye, or rum. And the only women who could be found in saloons were the dance hall girls. Things changed during Prohibition.

Right after Prohibition was passed, women received the right to vote. They felt that the United States was now changing into a modern world and women wanted to be in every part of it including the speakeasies.

Women's clothing styles changed. They got rid of stiff corsets and long skirts. They dared to wear dresses that showed their ankles and bare shoulders. They also wore stockings and garters that could hide a flask of liquor.

Speakeasy owners found that women were good for business. If there was music, the women wanted to dance and the men wanted to stay longer to dance with them. The longer the customers stayed, the more liquor the owner could sell. The speakeasies hired jazz musicians like Duke Ellington and Louis Armstrong and performers like Bojangles Robinson to entertain their customers. They also invented a new type of drink that would appeal to the ladies. It was called a cocktail. Bitter-tasting whiskey was mixed with fruit juices or soda pop and the new concoctions were an instant hit with men and women alike.

The speakeasies hired jazz musicians like Duke Ellington and Louis Armstrong and performers like Bojangles Robinson to entertain their customers.

The patrons of the speakeasies often drank their cocktails in china teacups. That way if the police raided the joint, the customer could gulp down the contents of the cup and claim they had just been "taking tea." Sometimes the excuse actually worked.

Despite the threat of raids and arrests, speakeasies became very popular—so popular that the owners needed a way to supply the growing demand for whiskey, rye, and rum. Their solution came from gangsters who had previously been working for labor gangs. Men like Al Capone and Dutch Schultz began to organize the bootleggers into a supply chain that could efficiently meet the need for illegal alcohol.

The gangsters were thrilled with Prohibition. It gave them a whole new way of making money and previously law-abiding citizens became their partners. Those who had run legal saloons and bars now found themselves part of organized crime, hiding from the police and selling the same liquor they had sold legally before Prohibition.

As gangster Al Capone said,

"All I ever did was sell beer and whiskey to our best people. All I ever did was to supply a demand that was pretty popular.**"**

Striped Pigs and Blind Tigers

When the sale of alcohol became illegal, several enterprising liquor salesmen decided make money another way. They wouldn't sell alcohol to their customers; instead, they would sell them a chance to see something unusual, like a pig with stripes or a blind tiger. Once the patron paid to "see" the animal, he or she was given a free drink of liquor. People started saying they were going to a "blind pig" when they were headed to visit a speakeasy.

FLAPPER FANTASTIC

Colleen Moore

Clara Bow

Mary Pickford

The world had seen nothing like it. Young women marched into hair salons with long, lustrous heads of hair and demanded to have it all cut off. They walked out with their hair chopped to chin length and mounds of hair left on the beauty parlor floor.

They took off their corsets and never put them back on, saying that they didn't want to wear such restrictive undergarments. It was impossible to dance the Charleston or the Shimmy in those old-fashioned corsets.

Instead, the girls wrapped strips of cloth around their chests to make them look as flat as possible. Then they did the most horrendous thing of all: They stopped wearing wool stockings and started wearing skirts that showed their ankles and sometimes even their calves! Parents and grandparents were horrified. These new fashions were an outrage. An abomination!

And then it got worse! Young women started smoking cigarettes and going to speakeasies to listen to that new jazz music. They drank bootleg whiskey and new-fangled cocktails. Preachers started giving sermons about the sins of the younger generation. Newspaper reporters loved the new fashions and the daring adventures of the young ladies. They started calling the girls "flappers" because of how they danced and flapped their arms about. Some people said they were like young birds flapping hard to break out of their parents' Victorian values.

Lois Long in her office at the New Yorker

Lipstick Long was one of the most famous flappers. Her real name was Lois Long, and she was hired by the brand-new magazine *The New Yorker* to write about the jazz clubs and speakeasies of New York. Lipstick took her job very seriously and spent every evening out on the town dancing and drinking in all of the best—and some of the worst—clubs. She would often go directly to *The New Yorker* office from her night out. She would arrive in the early hours of the morning wearing her party clothes and smelling of bootleg drinks. She would then strip to her slip and plop down at her typewriter to dash off her latest column for the paper.

Readers loved her stories about the newest alcoholic drinks like the Gin Rickey and Tom Collins. Whatever nightspot, singer, or jazz band that Lipstick recommended was sure to become all the rage with the "smart set"—popular young people.

Clara Bow was another very famous flapper. She was called the "It" girl of the 1920s. She was a gorgeous actress who appeared in 46 silent films and 11 "talkies" (films with sound). Because of her energy, beauty, and charming wit, she was said to have "It." And whatever "It" was, the public wanted more.

She shocked older audiences with her skimpy costumes, wild dancing, and bold make-up. But she was loved by young men and women and received more than 45,000 fan letters a month. And young women copied her clothing and hairstyles—the ultimate tribute.

The loose-fitting flapper dress like Clara Bow wore was much easier to sew than the old-fashioned skirts with bustles and lots of gathered material. Regular shop girls could afford to buy a pattern and material to sew their own fashionable flapper dress. They also crocheted their own tight-fitting knit caps in a style called a "cloche." It was the first time that women of modest incomes could actually afford to dress just like the movie stars.

Women against Prohibition

Parents and grandparents thought the birth of flapper girls meant an end to decent society. It was a dramatic change for the lives of women in the United States. They had received the right to vote, they felt they had the freedom to decide their own destinies, and they were ready to make the world their own. And they planned to have plenty of fun while they did it!

CAN YOU Do the Charleston?

Life magazine cover, 1928

The most popular dances of the 1920s were fast, furious, and full of energy. You can see what some of the stars of this era looked like in action in this clip, showing several different versions of the Charleston: https://www.youtube.com/watch?v=FQ7SNTSq-9o

GANGSTER SPEAK

"Move your get away sticks! There's a G-man packing heat in the juice joint."

"Let's blouse. I know where there's another blind pig."

"Okay, hop in the hayburner and we'll go."

Confused? Sounds like gibberish today, but in the Prohibition era, that conversation would have made perfect sense. Slang terms like "get away sticks," "let's blouse," and "hayburner" were a part of everyday conversation. During the 1920s and 1930s, gangsters used slang terms so they could talk in public without other people understanding what they were saying. Young people thought the gangster speak was fun and began using it in their everyday conversations.

Pretty soon, everybody understood that if you dressed up to go to a party you were "putting on your glad rags." Being the "cat's meow" or the "bee's knees" was a compliment, but being called a "palooka" or "rube" was an insult.

With a little practice, you can talk like the gangsters, bootleggers, and flappers of Prohibition days. Just use your noodle and the dictionary below. Pretty soon you'll be on the level with your gangster slang and able to beat your gums with every big cheese.

Slang Speak	Meaning
ab-so-lute-ly	affirmative
all wet	describes an erroneous idea or individual, as in "he's all wet"
all howl	emphatic response like, "You said it!"
applesauce	an expletive, similar to "horsefeathers," as in "Ah, applesauce!"
balled up	confused, messed up
baloney	nonsense
bank's closed	no kissing, as in "Sorry, Mac, the bank's closed"
bear cat	a hot-blooded or fiery girl
beat it	get out or get lost
beat your gums	chit-chat, talk
bee's knees	extraordinary person, thing, or idea; the ultimate; similar to "cat's meow"
beeswax	business, as in "none of your beeswax"
berries	something attractive or pleasing; similar to "bee's knees", as in "It's the berries"
big cheese	the most important or influential person; boss

Slang Speak	Meaning
blind pig	place where illegal alcohol was served, like a speakeasy; blind pigs had deceptive or "blank" fronts—often located in basements, behind peepholed doors, or in the back of legitimate businesses
caper	a criminal act or robbery
carry a torch	to have a crush on someone
cash	a kiss
cash or check	kiss now or later?
cat's meow	something splendid or stylish; the best or greatest, wonderful; similar to "bee's knees"; also used "cat's pajamas," "cat's whiskers," and "gnat's eyebrows"
chase yourself	go, get lost
cheaters	eyeglasses
check	kiss me later
chewing gum	double talk
copacetic	wonderful, fine, all right
coffin varnish	bootleg or homemade alcohol; also called "horse liniment," "stuff," and "tarantula juice"
crush	an infatuation
dame	a female
darb	an excellent person or thing
deb	a debutante
dick	a private investigator
doll	an attractive woman
dolled up	dressed up

Slang Speak	Meaning
don't take any wooden nickels	an expression that meant "don't do anything stupid" or "take care of yourself"
Dry	person against drinking and for Prohibition
dry up	shut up; get lost
earful	enough
egg	a person who lives the big life
fire extinguisher	a chaperone
flapper	a stylish, free-spirited young woman with short skirts and shorter hair
flat tire	a dull, boring, disappointing date; also known as a "pill," "pickle," "drag," "rag," or "oil can"
flyboy	a glamorous term for an aviator
fried	drunk
G-man	government agent
giggle water	alcohol
gin mill	a bar or establishment that sold liquor
glad rags	"going out on the town" clothes
goods	desired material, as in "you got the goods?"
goof	a bumbling person
goon	hoodlum
heel	scoundrel
hayburner	gas-guzzling car
heebie-jeebies	the jitters, anxiety
hit on all sixes	to hit on all six cylinders, 100% percent performance

Slang Speak	Meaning
hooch	bootleg liquor
hooey	nonsense
hoofer	dancer
iron	a motorcycle
jack	money
jake	all is okay, as in "everything is jake"
joe	coffee
juice joint	speakeasy
kale	money
know one's onions	know what you are talking about
lady legger	female bootlegger
let's blouse	let's get out of here
milquetoast	timid, mild person
mind your own potatoes	mind your own business
moonshine	bootleg alcohol
nifty	great, excellent
on the lam	fleeing from police
on the level	legitimate, honest
oyster fruit	pearls
packing heat	to carry a gun
palooka	man not considered to be very smart
pushover	person easily convinced of something
razz	to make fun of
ritzy	elegant (comes from the hotel name)
rube	"hick"; someone not considered to be very sophisticated
sap	a fool

Slang Speak	Meaning
sitting pretty	in a great position
swanky	ritzy
swell	wonderful
talkies	movies with sound
tomato	a female
Wet	someone who is against Prohibition and for the legalization of alcohol
wet blanket	a solemn person, a killjoy
whisper sister	female proprietor of a speakeasy
whoopee	to have a good time

Tarantula Juice?

During Prohibition people came up with lots of creative names for alcohol. Here are just a few of them: hooch, giggle water, moonshine, white lightning, panther sweat, coffin varnish, rotgut, bathtub gin, jorum of skee, tarantula juice, monkey rum, horse liniment, and brown plaid.

The Untouchables

THE SECRET
SIX
AND THE
UNTOUCHABLES

Al Capone

Everybody was scared of Al Capone. Nobody would testify against him or any of his men because they were afraid of getting the pineapple treatment (blown up by a grenade) or getting hit with a Tommy gun. People who talked bad about Capone or his men had a way of ending up dead.

But something had to be done to take Chicago back from the gangsters. Six of Chicago's wealthiest and most influential businessmen set up a secret meeting. They knew that in order to take down Capone and the other gangsters, they would have to find people who were willing to risk their lives. They needed a special team who would not give in to the gangsters' bribes and wouldn't be scared by the threat of death or torture. They needed a group of investigators who were untouchable.

The six businessmen knew their identities had to stay hidden or they would become targets of Capone and his men.

Nobody could know what they were planning, especially not reporters or the press. If word got out, their plan would be ruined and, worse, their friends and families might be kidnapped and killed.

They decided to hire Alexander G. Jamie as their director. Jamie had served as the chief special agent of the Prohibition bureau. He became known for his honesty by refusing huge bribes offered to him by gangsters. Jamie would be the public voice of the "Secret Six" and would keep the identities of the businessmen totally anonymous. The Secret Six would donate money to fund officers and missions, but they would never be in the public eye.

> One writer said that Ness and his team were so honest that they were "untouchable" by the gangsters. The nickname "The Untouchables" stuck.

Eliot Ness

Jamie, in turn, hired someone he trusted completely: his brother-in-law, Eliot Ness. Together, the two men began the search for an investigative team of lawmen who could not be bribed. They had to be single men because there was too much danger of them being killed in the line of duty. Jamie and Ness didn't want the responsibility of telling a wife or child they had lost their spouse or parent.

In the end, they selected nine men who were experienced in police and detective work and who had already resisted bribes from bootleggers and gangsters. Two of the men were chosen because they had experience as drivers. They needed to be able to tail the gangsters and make a fast getaway. Two more were chosen because they had experience with wiretaps. The team needed to be able to listen in on phone conversations without being detected. They also needed men who were good at tailing people, expert shots, and excellent in using disguises.

The team's first assignment was to make a dent in the cash flow of the gangsters. Some of the men posed as local policemen and pretended to be willing to take bribes from gangsters to "ignore" the stills that were operating in the Chicago neighborhoods. The gangsters believed them, and soon the team knew the location of 15 different stills that were pumping out more than 100 barrels of beer a day.

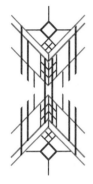

With that information, Ness and the rest of the men swarmed in and destroyed the stills. It cost the gangsters thousands of dollars in business and made them pay to set up new stills. Ness and his men became very good at tricking the gangsters, and reporters began writing about these new lawmen who were out to get Capone. One writer said that Ness and his team were so honest that they were "untouchable" by the gangsters. The nickname "The Untouchables" stuck.

But Capone and his men were disgusted with Ness. Several times, Ness and his men were shot at and there was a price on Ness' head. It didn't seem to bother any of them. They wore it as a badge of honor that they were marked by the gangsters for extermination.

The public of Chicago was behind Ness and the Untouchables. They wanted their city cleaned up and wanted the violence to stop. The Untouchables also had the financial backing of the Secret Six. One thing Ness did was to have a truck fitted with a special

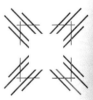

heavy-duty metal bumper that could be used to smash in the steel reinforced doors of the hidden breweries and stills. For months, the Untouchables worked to break down stills and arrest the gangsters.

It was a combination of the work by the Untouchables and the IRS that finally brought an end to Capone's hold on Chicago. When Capone was arrested and convicted for tax evasion, he tried to rule his group from behind bars. But the Untouchables had done so much damage to Capone's outfit that the gangsters were not as organized without him. They splintered off and argued and fought with each other. The end of Prohibition in 1933 meant a loss of their bootleg money. This further weakened the gangs and eventually helped free Chicago from the grip of Capone's men.

Cell block 8, cell 1:
Al Capone's cell at Alcatraz

The identities of the Secret Six are still not known for sure. It is believed that Harrison Barnard was one member. He was a trustee of the Shedd Aquarium. Julius Rosenwald, the president of Sears, Roebuck and Company was another member. There are other wealthy businessmen and lawyers who people suspect were members, but they have never been fully verified.

Izzy and Moe at a bar in New York City, 1935

IZZY AND MOE

When Isidor Einstein walked into the New York Prohibition Agency and asked for a job, the supervisor thought Izzy was joking. Izzy didn't look anything like a federal agent. He was short, fat, and middle-aged. The hiring agent laughed and told Izzy that he "wasn't the type" of man they were hiring. Izzy argued that was exactly why the agency should hire him. He didn't look like a big tough federal agent, so no one would suspect him. And in coming to America as an immigrant, Izzy had learned to speak six different languages. That impressed the federal agent, so he gave Izzy the job.

One of Izzy's first busts happened just as he suspected—because he didn't look anything like the big, muscled federal agents. He walked into a speakeasy wearing wrinkled pants and a rumpled shirt. He looked like any other working guy who was just stopping by to buy some bootleg whiskey except he was wearing his revenue agent's badge. He walked right up to the bartender and asked for a pint of whiskey. The bartender

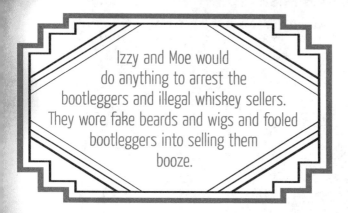

Izzy and Moe would
do anything to arrest the
bootleggers and illegal whiskey sellers.
They wore fake beards and wigs and fooled
bootleggers into selling them
booze.

looked at Izzy and his badge and laughed. He thought Izzy was wearing the badge as a joke, so he gave Izzy the whiskey. Then he asked where Izzy had gotten that crazy badge. Izzy clamped the handcuffs on the bartender and said, "I'll take you to the place it came from."

Soon, Izzy realized he could make more busts if he had a partner. He took his friend Moe Smith in to meet the hiring agent. Moe was a little taller than Izzy, but he was even fatter. He looked about as much like a federal agent as Izzy. Moe was hired.

For the next 5 years, Izzy and Moe were an amazing team of revenue detectives. They would do anything to arrest the bootleggers and illegal whiskey sellers. They wore fake beards and wigs and fooled bootleggers into selling them booze. They dressed up in tuxedos pretending to be royalty from a foreign country and arrested the poor guys who dared to serve them illegal drinks. They went to speakeasies dressed as musicians carrying instruments and then arrested every person in the joint.

Soon Izzy and Moe became front-page news. The public loved reading about their adventures. They cheered when they posed as fishermen and arrested bootleggers taking alcohol right off the boat. They laughed when Izzy pretended to nearly drown and Moe asked for a drink for his sopping wet friend. When the drink was provided, Izzy and Moe arrested everyone in the bar.

Izzy and Moe became so well-known that their pictures were posted inside speakeasies and bartenders were warned to never serve them and to shut down if the agents were spotted in the neighborhood. That didn't slow down Izzy and Moe—they just dreamed up new disguises.

One afternoon, they put on football uniforms, covered themselves with mud, and marched into a speakeasy shouting that they were there to celebrate the end of the season. When the bartender served them their drinks, Izzy said, "I got sad news for you."

The bartender, thinking it was a joke, asked, "What news?"

Izzy said, "You're pinched." And he pulled out the handcuffs.

Besides using disguises, Izzy also created an invention that helped him catch the bootleggers. It was a rubber tube attached to a funnel and a storage bag. Izzy hid the tube and funnel near his throat under his overcoat. When he sat down at a bar, he would pretend to drink the alcohol, but would instead pour it into the funnel. When Izzy arrested the bootlegger, he had the evidence hidden under his coat.

The press was always ready to accompany Izzy and Moe on their raids, and the men were happy to tell them their plans. It sold papers for the newsmen, and it made Izzy and Moe famous. Izzy never carried a firearm and Moe carried a gun, but never used it. They preferred to use their wit and charm. They made 4,932 arrests and 95% of the people they arrested were convicted. They confiscated more than 5 million gallons of liquor with an estimated value of $15 million. On their "best" night they conducted 71 raids in less than 12 hours. They had the highest arrest rate of any Prohibition agents.

Such an impressive record should be a cause for celebration and rewards, but instead of receiving honors for the best arrest record, they were fired. After 5 years of service, they were laid off because their supervisors were jealous of all the press and publicity they had received. The Revenue Service fired its two best agents.

Izzy and Moe didn't protest their firing, although they were disappointed to lose their jobs. They both went into the insurance business and became successful businessmen. Sometimes they even sold insurance policies to people they had arrested in the past. Izzy died in 1938 at the age of 57. Moe lived to be 73 and died in 1960. In 1985, a television movie was made about their adventures, starring Jackie Gleason and Art Carney.

RADIO
CODE BREAKER

Rumrunners and bootleggers used coded radio messages to communicate from land to ship. Radios were a fairly new invention and were quite expensive, but bootlegging was a profitable business. The smugglers had the latest technology and they also used codes to fool anyone who might be listening.

The U.S. Coast Guard heard all of the new chatter on its radios, but it didn't make any sense. The Coast Guard knew

Elizebeth Smith Friedman

it was the smugglers talking to each other, but didn't have a clue as to what they were saying. The Coast Guard tried its hand at decoding, but had no success.

In 1923, the Coast Guard turned over the messages to the U.S. Treasury Department, hoping that it could make sense of the strange messages. The work was given to Elizebeth Smith Friedman. Elizebeth was an expert at cryptanalysis and had done

The bootleggers had to be surprised when the Coast Guard began stopping their shipments. They figured that someone was cracking their codes, so they made them more complicated. They were still easy for Elizebeth.

work for the military during World War I. When she got hold of the bootleggers' codes, she found them to be quite simple and had them solved almost immediately.

The bootleggers had to be surprised when the Coast Guard began stopping their shipments. They figured that someone was cracking their codes, so they made them more complicated. They were still easy for Elizebeth. She cracked the new codes. She cracked the next round of codes. She kept cracking codes until Prohibition was repealed. Eventually, she cracked more than 12,000 smugglers' messages and testified in numerous smuggling cases. Her work resulted in convictions against 35 different bootleg ringleaders.

Elizebeth went on to work as a codebreaker during World War II. She and her husband worked together to capture Americans who were spying for Japan. She died in 1980 at the age of 88, having helped capture spies and smugglers for more than three decades.

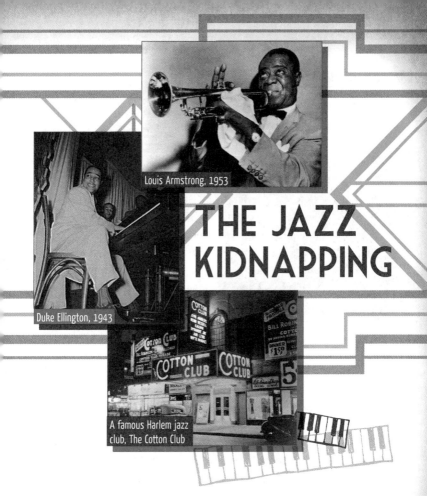

Louis Armstrong, 1953

Duke Ellington, 1943

A famous Harlem jazz club, The Cotton Club

THE JAZZ KIDNAPPING

Gangsters, flappers, and bootleggers all agreed on one thing: They loved jazz music. It was the latest music craze, and it was totally different than hymns, marching band music, or opera. The rhythm was fast and the music slid up and down the scale like a snake swimming in a river. It was the music of choice in most speakeasies and the best jazz players were found in the hidden bars and saloons of Harlem, a neighborhood in New York City.

Fats Waller, 1938

Fats Waller was one of the most famous jazz pianists during the 1920s. He was born Thomas Wright Waller, but his friends called him Fats. He started playing piano when he was just 6 years old, and by the time he was 18, he had already recorded two piano solos.

Everybody wanted to hear Fats play the piano. The clubs he played in were always packed and the concerts he gave were sold out. In 1926, Fats had just finished working the night at a speakeasy in Chicago. He was tired and ready to fall into bed, but when he stepped outside the club, he was met by men holding guns. They ordered Fats to get into the waiting car.

Fats was terrified. He had read about the Chicago gangs and how when they "took you for a ride," it didn't end well. He was sure he was going to be killed. The car stopped at the Hawthorne Inn and the men ordered Fats to get out. They marched him inside the building. Fats didn't know what was going to happen to him. Maybe he would be shot to death in a dark, empty room?

But when he walked inside the hotel, he saw bright lights, loud music, and lots of people laughing and drinking bootleg alcohol. It looked like the club he had just left. One of the guys with a gun shoved him toward a waiting piano and told him to start playing. Fats did what he was told. When he finished the first song, he saw a man standing and clapping loudly. Fats noticed the scars on the man's face. It was none other than Al (Scarface) Capone.

Fats Waller had been kidnapped to be the entertainment for Al Capone's 27th birthday party. Fats realized he wasn't going to be killed and settled in to make the best of things. He played all of the songs requested and spent nearly 3 days partying with and playing for Al and the Capone gang.

When the 3-day party was over, Al sent him home in a limousine. Fats was full of fancy food and rare champagne, and his pockets were stuffed with thousands of dollars in tip money. That was the one and only performance Fats gave for Capone.

The jazz music of Fats Waller and his friends lives on today. Two of his most popular songs "Ain't Misbehavin'" and "Honeysuckle Rose" were inducted into the Grammy Hall of Fame.

Ain't Misbehavin'

You can watch a video of Fats Waller playing his famous music at: https://www.youtube.com/watch?v=PSNPpssruFY

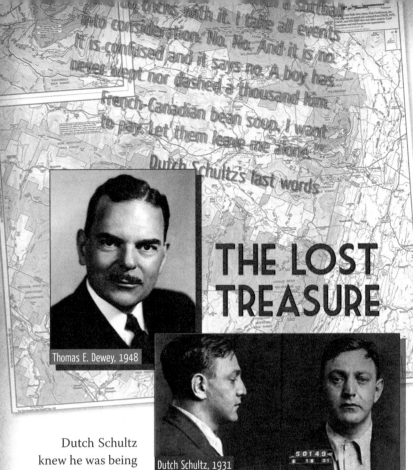

into consideration. No. No. And it is no it is confused and it says no. A boy has never went nor dashed a thousand kim. French-Canadian bean soup. I want to pay. Let them leave me alone.

Dutch Schultz's last words

Thomas E. Dewey, 1948

THE LOST TREASURE

Dutch Schultz, 1931

Dutch Schultz knew he was being hunted by the FBI. They'd been following him to every speakeasy and gin joint in town. The G-Men had people watching his bootleg deliveries. They were staking out his gambling houses and shadowing his bodyguards. And most pesky of all was that New York prosecutor, Thomas Dewey. He needed to mind his own business.

Schultz knew what to do with enemies. He'd sent several rivals to their grave with a round of Tommy gun fire. One enemy he hung up by his thumbs on a meat hook. Dutch Schultz was not a nice guy. However, he was very wealthy. He had been running bootleg operations throughout Prohibition. He also managed gambling houses and several other illegal enterprises. He knew it was only a matter of time before the Feds or Dewey's men arrested him.

Schultz had seen what happened to other gangsters when they got caught. They served out their sentence for bootlegging or tax evasion and got out of jail in a couple of years only to find that another gangster had taken over their territory. They ended up broke and without any way back into the bootleg business. Schultz was determined that he was not going to be like those other saps. He was going to outsmart the Feds. His plan was to hide a portion of his cash, jewelry, and goods where no one would ever find it. Then, when he got out of jail, Dutch Schultz would still be a wealthy man.

But avoiding jail altogether would be even better. Maybe if he could get rid of that legal eagle Thomas Dewey he wouldn't get caught. That was Schultz's master plan: Gun down Dewey and then his problem

Police lineup of gangsters Eddie Diamond, left, Legs Diamond, Gurrah Shapiro, and Lucky Luciano

would go away. Schultz talked to some of his fellow gangsters like Legs Diamond and Lucky Luciano, trying to convince them that if they helped him get rid of Dewey, then they would all be safer. Luciano and Diamond thought Schultz had gone crazy. Killing a big name prosecutor like Thomas Dewey would bring on the wrath of the whole New York Police Department. They told Schultz to forget the harebrained scheme.

But Schultz was sure that this was the way he could save himself, so he made plans with some other men to try to assassinate Dewey. When Diamond and Luciano heard about this, they were furious. They decided they had to get rid of Dutch Schultz.

A hit was put out on Dutch Schultz, and on October 23, 1935, he was gunned down in a tavern in New Jersey. He was shot in the spleen, stomach, colon, and liver, but didn't die immediately. He spent nearly 24 hours in a New Jersey hospital going in and out of consciousness.

A police stenographer was assigned to sit at his bedside and write down everything that Schultz said. Much of it didn't make sense. He was delirious with fever and near death, but part of his conversation intrigued reporters. He rambled on about money in a box and how nobody would know where to find it. He talked about going to the woods and hiding something. And then said that people would be surprised to know what was hidden in the woods.

His death made newspaper headlines across the country and reporters included the notes the stenographer had made. Soon the world was talking about the possibility of finding Dutch Schultz's lost treasure.

In his deathbed mutterings, Schultz had talked about the woods in Phoenicia, NY. That was enough of a clue for hundreds of treasure hunters. They began scouring the woods near Phoenicia. People dug holes, explored caves, and looked in every crack and crevice they could find. One man even hired a backhoe to dig in a spot he was sure held the treasure. But in 80 years of hunting, no one has ever found Dutch Schultz's lost treasure. Of course that doesn't mean it's not out there. It just means that treasure hunters still have hope.

1940 Ford bootlegging car

One of the first NASCAR drivers, The Red Byron, 1939

INVENTION

OF NASCAR

One of the first NASCAR races

For years, it was a secret past that nobody wanted to talk about. The truth is that NASCAR was invented by bootleggers.

During the Prohibition years, moonshiners in the Appalachian Mountains would make their illegal alcohol and pour it into jars. They then packed it carefully into boxes, put it into the trunk of a car, and covered it with a pile of blankets or coats. Then it was up to the driver to get the moonshine safely to town and get it sold.

Driving the moonshine was the most dangerous job. The drivers had to watch out for Prohibition officers who were looking to arrest them. They were driving on winding roads that were unpaved and full of potholes. They also had to try not to break the jars of shine.

In order to be able to outrun the officers, the moonshiners began tinkering with their motors. They made the engines more powerful. Then they began altering the frames of the car. They took out

Pretty soon, the moonshiners were outrunning the police.

metal in some places to make it lighter. They reinforced metal in other places to make the car able to withstand the rough roads.

Pretty soon, the moonshiners were outrunning the police. Their cars were faster and could survive high speeds on rough roads. Some of the moonshiners considered racing the police to be a great form of entertainment. They loved the speed and excitement. They began bragging about how fast their cars were to the other moonshiners. Of course, the braggers were asked to prove it and a race was arranged.

People showed up to watch the moonshiners race each other and bet on who the winners would be. Enterprising landowners plowed circular tracks on their ground and invited the drivers to race. Crowds showed up, and money was made on betting and selling some of the moonshine.

Businessmen realized that people would be willing to pay to watch the drivers race. They built real racetracks with grandstand seating so people could watch in comfortable seats. They added concession stands and lured the best drivers by offering prize money to winners.

Big Bill France

In 1947, Big Bill France held a meeting with the drivers, mechanics, and car owners to standardize the race rules. It was from this meeting that the National Association for Stock Car Auto Racing was formed. In 1948, NASCAR held its first official race on the sands of Daytona Beach, FL. Many of the drivers and mechanics were still involved in the moonshine trade.

As NASCAR became more and more popular, large corporations paid to sponsor drivers and the cars. The corporations didn't want anyone to talk about the history of the races. It would be bad for business to mention the moonshine heritage. Over the years, the public forgot about the moonshiners and their wild races with the law. NASCAR became a respectable law-abiding sport. But the truth is, it all began with moonshiners being chased by Prohibition agents.

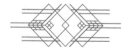

GET THE GOODS

Slang Code

Both gangsters and policemen wanted to keep information to themselves. They didn't want anyone listening in on their conversation and understanding what was going on.

The gangsters used slang words or made-up terms to fool the police. The police used code words to fool the gangsters. You can make up your own secret words to keep people (like your little sister or brother) from spying on you and your friends.

First think about what you DON'T want people to know and make up a word or phrase that only you and your friends will understand. For example, you might want to tell your friends to meet you at school at 8 a.m. To fool your little brother, you can use made-up words or phrases to give the information. You can substitute the phrase *fool's tool* for school. Instead of 8 a.m. you can say *prime time.* So your sentence would be "*Make it prime time at the fool's tool.*" Rhyming words help make it hard for others to understand and it's fun. Repeating consonants at the beginning of words also makes it easier to remember and use the code.

Try out some of these phrases or make up your own.

Word	Code Phrase
school	fool's tool
home	shlub club
store	sly buy
dog	howl pal
cat	mouser douser
friend	great mate
park	game plain
mom	gravy lady
dad	big bloke
teacher	rooter tutor
coach	drill thrill
backyard	mean green

GET THE GOODS

Marble-Powered Race Car

You can create your own race car with index cards and a marble. Once you have it moving, you can experiment and see how to make it even faster. Build a couple and race with your friends. Who knows? You may be a future NASCAR driver!

Materials

- ❑ 4 x 6 index cards
- ❑ Tape
- ❑ Scissors
- ❑ File folder
- ❑ Marble
- ❑ Tape measure

Fold the index card in half like a hot dog bun. This will be the body of your car. At the front edge of the car, cut a triangle off the top and bottom so the car will not drag as it moves along the floor. You can decorate your car to look like a NASCAR racer.

Next, you will need to make the ramp. Take the file folder and bend the bottom of the folder in, to create an inverted V shape. This will be the track for the marble. Fold the side edges of the folder so it sits evenly on the floor. Once you have it adjusted the way you want, tape the edges together.

Set the ramp on a smooth floor. Place the race car at the very bottom of the ramp. Then roll the marble down the ramp and into the car. Mark the distance the car traveled. Try it again and see if you can make your car go farther. You may want to build ramps of different heights and see which ramp makes your car move the greatest distance.

Car: **Ramp:**

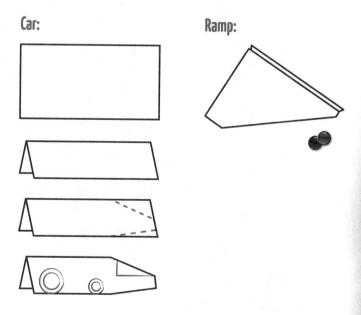

SHOOTOUTS
& SCOUNDRELS

Members of the The Purple Gang, 1931

THE PURPLE GANG

The Bernstein Brothers

Abe   Joe   Ray   Izzy

They started out as young pickpockets, swiping wallets, pocket watches, and purses from people in the crowds of Detroit. They graduated to armed robbery, kidnapping, and extortion. Led by the four Bernstein brothers, the Purple Gang became notorious for its willingness to beat up its enemies.

Legend has it that the gang got its name because neighborhood citizens said the boys were "rotten, purple, like the color of bad meat." Their violence scared off older, less violent gangs, and by the 1920s, the Purple Gang ruled Detroit.

The Purple Gang began the business of bootlegging 3 years before most other gangs. The state of Michigan had passed the Damon Act of 1916 and made liquor illegal in 1917. With Canada making alcohol just across the border, it was simple for the Purple Gang to set up a bootlegging system to supply the citizens of Detroit and much of Michigan with whiskey and rum. By the time the rest of America joined Prohibition, the Purple Gang already had established suppliers and delivery networks.

> By the time the rest of America joined Prohibition, the Purple Gang already had established suppliers and delivery networks.

Word of the Purple Gang's excellent bootleg system reached Al Capone in Chicago. Scarface himself contacted the Purple Gang and worked to negotiate a deal between his outfit and the gang. But Capone never fully trusted the men in the Purple Gang and considered them too violent. The gang was known to order hits—or assassinations—on anyone it felt had "crossed" the gang.

One person they wanted killed was Joseph Kennedy, the father of future president John F. Kennedy. Joe Kennedy was running a smuggling operation of his own—buying liquor through his connections in Ireland and England and smuggling it through Canada. The Purple Gang felt that Kennedy was stepping on its turf and for that he should be killed, so the gang put out a contract on his life.

Kennedy was warned about the contract and managed to work through Chicago gangster Diamond Joe Esposito to have the contract lifted. Kennedy managed to avoid being killed by the Purple Gang, but many others were not so lucky.

Besides running liquor, the Purple Gang got involved in the Detroit labor unions. They established a fake Cleaners and Dryers Union. The dryers and cleaners of the city had to "pay dues" to the Purple Gang or they would be harassed and assaulted. The gang threw stink bombs into laundry facilities, shattered windows, and smashed the equipment of any company that did not cooperate. When two companies refused to pay, their businesses were bombed and two of the businessmen were murdered. The citizens of Detroit were terrified of the Purple Gang and everyone was afraid to testify against the members, believing that their families would be hurt or killed. Although some of the gang members were arrested and charged for the "Cleaners and Dryers War," they were later acquitted of the charges.

It wasn't until 1931 that the police were able to stop the Purple Gang and only because the gang got so brazen that it was not careful. The Purple Gang was in a turf war with another smaller gang and decided to simply eliminate its leaders. The gang arranged a meeting with Sol Levine as a go-between. Sol knew men in both gangs and was willing to help set up a peace conference. On the day of the meeting, the Purple Gang members showed up, but they didn't have peace on their agenda. They sprayed the room with gunshots and killed everyone but Sol. Sol was spared only because he had friends in the Purple Gang. But that was a big mistake for the Purple Gang: The shooting scared Sol so much that he thought he was safer confessing everything to the police. Sol Levine

Members of the The Purple Gang arrested, 1931

identified the four leaders of the Purple Gang and had to be guarded by 10 policemen so that he would not be killed before or during the trial. The leaders of the Purple Gang were finally brought to justice and sentenced to life in prison.

The Detroit police were ecstatic. They had broken the Purple Gang and felt that their city was a much safer place.

VALENTINE'S DAY MASSACRE

MASSACRE 7 OF MORAN GANG

The Chicago Daily News, February 14, 1929

Actual weapons used in the Valentine's Day Massacre, 1929

Bugs Moran

Bugs Moran was running late. He was supposed to meet some of his gang at a garage on Clark Street in Chicago. It was a cold Valentine's Day, and the tall Moran had his hat pulled down against the wind and was wearing a heavy winter dress coat. He looked like any other Chicago businessman, but he wasn't. He was the leader of the North Side Gang, the biggest rival of Al Capone's outfit.

Moran and Capone had been at war with each other for years. Capone believed Moran's men were stealing his shipments of whiskey from Detroit. Moran accused Capone of trying to take over the North Side's territory. Just like in a war of countries, the men tried to settle things with guns.

This Valentine's Day, Moran was going to put one over on Capone. The day before, Moran had received a call that a truckload of highjacked whiskey was coming in from Detroit.

The killing was decimating to Bugs Moran's gang. In a few minutes, he lost his second in command, two of his main enforcers, his bookkeeper, two friends, and his mechanic.

Moran had to have been happy that he was once again cutting into Capone's profits. He told some of his men to meet at the garage at 10:30 to unload and stash the shipment.

But Moran left his apartment later than he planned. Walking with Ted Newberry, the men spotted a police car at the garage. They figured the police were there to check up on them again. Better to wait until the police were done, they thought, turning back and heading to a coffee shop.

Across the street, the landlady, Mrs. Jeanette Landesman, heard what she thought was gunfire and a dog howling. She looked out her window and saw two police officers marching three men out of the garage and into the police car. Would Chicago ever get rid of all the gang violence?

The dog continued howling after the police car had driven away. Mrs. Landesman asked one of her tenants to go over and see what was wrong with the poor dog. The man ran back to the house, his face white. He shouted for Mrs. Landesman to call for the police—the garage was full of dead men!

Inside the garage was a horrific sight. Seven men had been lined up against the wall and sprayed with bullets from machine guns. When the real police arrived, six of the

TOP SECRET FILES GANGSTERS *AND* BOOTLEGGERS

men were already dead. Only Frank Gusenberg was still alive. He had been shot 14 times, but was still conscious. The police tried to question him. They asked who had shot him, but Frank replied,

Frank Gusenberg

⟶ **"No one shot me."** ⟵

He died 3 hours later without telling who had attacked him and his partners.

When Bugs Moran found out what had happened to his gang members, he was furious. He immediately accused Al Capone of ordering the hit, but Al Capone was at his home in Florida. When newspaper reporters contacted Capone, he told them that the only man who killed like that was Bugs Moran.

Bugs Moran was probably right. But the murders were never solved by the police or tried in the courts. Detectives and reporters have pieced together what they believe happened on that Valentine's Day, but there were no people willing to testify against Al Capone. And no one was willing to identify the men they saw come out of the garage.

Detectives believed that five men outfitted a car to look just like a police car. Two of the men were dressed in police uniforms and three of the men were in dress suits. The men went into the garage and confronted the North Side Gang members. The men thought it was just a simple police raid. They cooperated and lined up against the wall. Then the men in suits opened fire with machine guns. In seconds, the North Side Gang members were dead.

To fool the people in the neighborhood, the three men dressed in street clothes came out with their hands up and the men dressed as policemen used the guns to prod them into the police car. They drove away before anyone suspected anything.

The killing was decimating to Bugs Moran's gang. In a few minutes, he lost his second in command, two of his main enforcers, his bookkeeper, two friends, and his mechanic. For Al Capone, it was a victory. He became the undisputed king of Chicago crime, but he also became Public Enemy No. 1.

The people of Chicago were horrified at such a grisly crime and authorities became determined to catch Al Capone any way they could. It was the beginning of the end for his gang, but Capone had no idea.

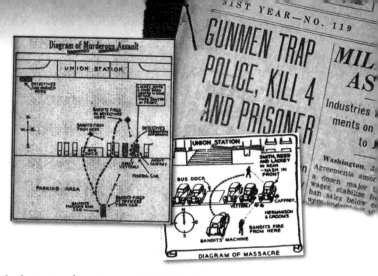

Diagram of Murderous Assault

UNION STATION

GUNMEN TRAP POLICE, KILL 4 AND PRISONER

MIL AS

Industries ments on to

Washington, Agreements amor a dozen major ban sales below

DIAGRAM OF MASSACRE

KANSAS CITY
MASSACRE

Frank Nash

Frank Nash was a nasty piece of work. He was convicted of murder for the first time in 1913 at the age of 26, but was pardoned when he volunteered to fight in World War I. After serving just a few months in the war, he returned home and went back to a life of crime, robbing more than 200 banks. He was considered a mastermind at planning and helped organize several prison escapes for gangster friends. He even managed to escape prison himself in 1930. He remained free until two Oklahoma lawmen caught up with him at a cigar store in Hot Springs, AR, in June of 1933.

The lawmen were anxious to get Nash in to the hands of federal authorities. Because Nash was known for masterminding bank robberies and escapes, the lawmen were taking no chances. They escorted Nash themselves on a train to Kansas City and made arrangements for FBI agents to meet them there. They planned to have a two-car convoy to escort Nash back to jail. They didn't want anything to go wrong.

The conspirators

Adam Richetti

Charles "Pretty Boy" Floyd

Vernon Miller

But friends of Nash heard about his capture and hatched a plan to rescue him from the FBI. They decided to meet Nash's train at the station in Kansas City and grab him away from the authorities. The gangsters were armed with machine guns and were sure they could rescue their buddy. What could go wrong? Everything.

When Nash arrived at the Kansas City station, he was guarded by seven officers. Two of them carried shotguns and the rest had pistols. They made their way through the lobby of the station watching to see if anything looked suspicious. Once outside, they went to one of the officer's cars and ordered Nash to get in. They put him in the front seat so they could keep an eye on him. Four of the officers were going to guard Nash in the car and the other two would follow behind in a separate car.

Suddenly a shout came from a green car parked a few feet away. "Let 'em have it!" a man shouted. The officers saw three men running with machine guns. The machine guns began firing, and within seconds, three of the officers had been killed. So had Frank Nash.

His would-be rescuers had not counted on him being in the front seat. The men ran to the car and yelled, "They're all dead. Let's get out of here!"

In reality, three of the lawmen did survive the attack and lived to testify against the gangsters. Four of the planners and one gunman were convicted and sent to jail. The two other gunmen were killed, one by another gangster and one by police. It was one instance where crime definitely did not pay.

GUN MOLLS

Behind every great gangster stood his gun moll. Okay, maybe not always *behind* him, but somewhere near him. During the 1920s, girlfriends of gangsters were often as famous as the gangsters themselves. Reporters called them gun molls, and the women were photographed in glamorous clothes wearing the latest hairstyles.

There is debate as to why they were called molls. Some believe it was the shortened form of the name Molly, which was slang for a girl. Others believe it was because women in the 1920s were often called "dolls." Only these dolls carried guns in their purses or hidden in their clothing or coats.

Mae Capone, wife of Al Capone, shielding her face after visiting her husband at Alcatraz, 1936

Some of the molls like Mae Capone never carried guns and weren't involved in the gangsters' life of crime. They were most guilty of turning a blind eye to what their boyfriends or husbands did as a living. Mae Capone never approved of what Al did for a living and told their son not to follow in his father's footsteps because Al had broken her heart. Sonny listened to his mother and stayed out of the crime scene.

The molls of the Dillinger Gang were far from innocent. They helped hide the infamous gang from the police after it committed a string of bank robberies. They also helped the men escape prison and covered them in shootouts. Most of them served prison sentences at the same time as their boyfriends.

Mary Northern Kinder

Mary Northern Kinder looked like a sweet young mother. She wore her hair in a short bob with waves, just like the style of the day worn by many women. She didn't look like a woman who would help a gang of men break out of prison, but she did—and she drove the getaway car. This crime made her one of only two women on the Chicago Public Enemies list in 1933.

Blanche Barrow

Blanche Barrow was a member of the same gang as Bonnie and Clyde. Blanche not only carried guns, she knew how to fire them and used guns in shootouts with the police. She also helped the Barrow Gang in an armed robbery. When the police caught up with Blanche, she didn't go quietly. Blanche fought to the end and was blinded in one eye during the shootout. She spent 6 years in prison for her crimes.

Some gangster molls paid for their loyalty with their lives. Elfrieda Rigus was the longtime girlfriend of Frank McErlane, a Chicago bootlegger who often drank too much of his own illegal alcohol. McErlane was known as a very tough gangster. Once when he was in the hospital recovering from shotgun wounds, three men from another gang burst into the hospital and tried to kill him. McErlane calmly pulled an automatic gun out from under his pillow and returned fire. He missed, but scared the men away. The next day, the men were found dead on a hit ordered by McErlane. Unfortunately for his girlfriend, McErlane got rid of her just as ruthlessly.

One autumn afternoon, McErlane was out for a drive with his girlfriend when they got into an argument. Instead of settling it peacefully, it is believed that McErland shot and killer her. Even though the police were sure that he was the one who murdered Elfrieda, they could not prove it and McErlane never went to jail for the shooting.

John Dillinger and Evelyn Frechette

Not all gangster molls ended up dead. John Dillinger's girlfriend, Evelyn Frechette, was a beautiful young woman who fell madly in love with the bank robber. She stayed with him through bank robberies, shootouts, and cross-country runs from the police.

When she was caught, Frechette was sentenced to 2 years and one day in prison. While serving her time, she wrote a booklet about crime. Once she was out, she published the brochure and sold it to help warn others about the consequences of crime. She also joined a group of family members of criminals who were touring the country speaking about why "Crime Does Not Pay."

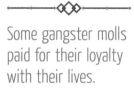

Some gangster molls paid for their loyalty with their lives.

Frechette felt it was her way of warning other young people to stay away from crime and the glamorous, but dangerous life of a gun moll.

THE MAN IN THE GREEN HAT

George Cassiday, 1930

Most of the people working in Washington, DC, just called him the "man in the green hat." During the 1920s, he was a familiar face in the halls of Congress. He arrived early every morning, wearing his jaunty green fedora and disappeared down to his office in the basement. At night, he would leave with the rest of the workers, sometimes tipping his famous green hat to the ladies he met.

But what was his job?

And what was his name?

Many people never knew. And those who knew didn't talk about it.

His name was George L. Cassiday Sr. and he was a bootlegger. Actually he was *the* bootlegger for the Congressmen and Senators of the United States of America—the same legislators who had voted Prohibition into law in 1919. While all of America was banned from buying and selling alcohol, the legislators gave Cassiday and his green hat an office and plenty of business.

Cassiday got started in bootlegging after he returned home from serving in World War I. Jobs were hard to come by for veterans. The job he had left behind for the war had been given to someone else. Cassiday had a wife and young children and needed a way to earn some money.

A friend of Cassiday said there was an easy way to earn money by providing bootlegged alcohol for a couple of Congressmen. Cassiday thought his friend was joking, but he was serious. Cassiday agreed to get the Congressmen their moonshine, and the men were so grateful that they told other people about Casiday's little "service" of providing bootleg. Word spread that Cassiday was discreet and charged a fair price. Soon, he had a full-blown business.

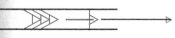

While all of America was banned from buying and selling alcohol, the legislators gave Cassiday and his green hat an office and plenty of business.

Everyday, Cassiday would enter the Congress building with bottles hidden in his brief case. He carried in all he could, but there was just too much demand from the legislators. Cassiday couldn't carry enough in, so one of the lawmakers figured out a solution. He found an empty office in the basement and assigned it to Cassiday.

This made his job much less complicated, and it made life simpler for the legislators, too. Now they had an even easier time breaking the law and buying bootleg liquor. All they had to do was send a secretary down to the office to pick up their order. Legislators were never searched when they were leaving the building, so they could carry home all the liquor they could squeeze into their bags and briefcases.

Now the most difficult task for Cassiday was getting the liquor to the office. At first, he had to travel to New York City by train to pick up the illegal alcohol. He would take two large suitcases and fill them with bootleg and then ride the train back to Washington, DC. This was the most dangerous part of his job. He knew most of the legislators weren't going to turn him in, but if he got caught hauling suitcases of alcohol, he would be headed to jail.

Once he set a suitcase down too hard and a bottle cracked. A man walking by smiled at Cassiday and said, "Buddy, your clothes are leaking." Cassiday went to a men's room and washed out his suitcase so it wouldn't give him away by smelling of liquor. He managed to deliver the rest of the bottles unbroken.

For 5 years, Cassiday took orders and delivered alcohol to the Congressmen in Washington, DC, but in 1925, someone ratted him out. Cassiday was stopped by the police with one of his suitcases of liquor. He was sentenced to 6 months of jail time. When he was released, he learned that he was banned from the House of Representatives building.

But fortunately for Cassiday, the legislators liked his work so much that they set him up with a new office in the basement of the Senate. For 5 more years, Cassiday supplied illegal liquor to the highest profile people in Washington, DC.

He estimated that four out of five legislators drank illegal alcohol. Both Republicans and Democrats who bought from him; people who had voted against Prohibition and those who had voted for it. Some of the legislators tried to explain their actions. They said that even if they didn't believe in Prohibition, they knew their constituents wanted Prohibition passed, so they voted for it anyway.

"The MAN in the GREEN HAT Capitol Tipplers Had Weakness For Rye, Bourbon, Says Cassiday

One of George Cassiday's five-part series for *The Washington Post*, 1930

In 1930, an election year, Cassiday was caught delivering an order by a Prohibition officer. He was sentenced to 18 months in jail, and his bootlegging career was over. But Cassiday wasn't going out without telling his story: He wrote a five-part series for *The Washington Post* newspaper, which appeared just one week before the 1930 elections.

Cassiday's story illustrated the hypocrisy of the legislators who voted for Prohibition, but bought liquor for themselves. It was one more reason for unhappy constituents to vote out the Republicans who were in the majority and vote in the Democrats who wanted to repeal Prohibition.

Historians today credit Cassiday's newspaper articles for helping bring an end to Prohibition in the United States. As for the man in the green hat, he never went back to bootlegging. Because of his connections, Cassiday was able to sign in to the jail each day and go home to sleep every night for the 18-month sentence. When he had served his time, he went to work at a shoe factory and later worked for several hotels in Washington, DC. He died in 1967 at the age of 74. In 2012, the first post-Prohibition distillery in Washington, DC, named its gin after him: Green Hat Gin.

GET THE GOODS
Just Kidding Around

Flappers and bootleggers all seemed to be having fun at the speakeasies and gin joints of the 1920s, but what did the kids of this time period do for entertainment?

Outdoor games were the same as most kids play now. They liked baseball and kickball, and if there was no ball available, they played Kick the Can. Indoors, kids played board games and paper-and-pencil games. Radio broadcasts were a new invention in 1920, but by 1928, kids could listen to detective and Western shows on the radio (if they had their parent's permission). They also listened to news broadcasts about the gangsters and the FBI's Public Enemy No. 1: Al Capone.

You can try some of the games kids played in the 1920s. All you will need is a pencil, some paper, and a group of friends.

WHY?

You will need a group of four or five people. Give each person a piece of paper and a pencil. Every person writes a question at the top of their paper. The question must start with "Why." For example, "Why do pigs like mud?"

Then, fold the top of the paper over to hide the question. Everyone should pass his or her paper to the left.

Without looking at the question, the players will all write an answer starting with the word "Because." For example, you might write, "Because bees like flowers." Pass the paper around until everyone has written an answer on each sheet. Then read out all of the questions and their answers and enjoy how funny they can get!

Foldovers

One entertainment for kids in the 1920s was reading the comic strip in the newspaper. They loved reading about the adventures of Little Orphan Annie or Buster Brown. Kids would draw their own comics or play a game called Foldovers to make crazy cartoon pictures.

To play Foldovers, you will need two or three friends. Give each person a piece of paper and a pencil. Fold each piece of paper into three equal sections. Then, unfold the paper so you can see the creases that mark each section. Have each person draw a head on the top section. It can be as crazy or silly as you want. Then fold the top section over so that it cannot be seen.

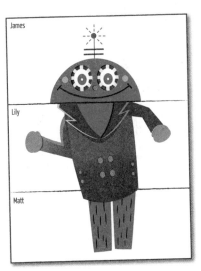

Have everybody pass their papers to the left. Next, each person will draw a chest, stomach, and arms on the middle section. It can be the arms of a person, alien, or dinosaur. Whatever you want—be creative! Fold it over again.

Pass the papers to the left a third time. Now on the bottom section of the paper, draw the legs and feet of the creature. Again, be as crazy as you want. Then pass the paper to the left once more. This time, everyone opens up his or her paper to reveal the strange comic creation.

Read the Real Comics

First Little Orphan Annie
Sunday page, 1924

You can read samples of the "Little Orphan Annie" and "Buster Brown" comic strips on the Internet: http://xroads.virginia. edu/~ug00/lambert/ images/bb1.jpg or http://xroads.virginia. edu/~ug00/lambert/ images/loa1.jpg

MOST
WANTED

SCARFACE

Al Capone, Scarface, 1930

Al Capone's criminal record, 1932

Al Capone's scars

The girl was pretty. Alphonse was rude. The girl's brother made Alphonse pay.

That's the real reason Al Capone had three scars on his face. He sometimes told people he got the scars from fighting in the Great War. Sometimes he told them he had an accident as a child. But like many things in Al Capone's life, those were the lies.

When Al Capone was a kid, he lived in Brooklyn, NY, with his parents and eight brothers and sisters. He was smart and made pretty good grades, but he had trouble following the rules in his strict Catholic school. He dropped out of school at 14 and went to work. He worked for a while at a candy store, he set pins at a bowling alley, and he was a cutter in a book bindery, but those jobs, just like school, were too boring. Al Capone wanted excitement. He also wanted money.

He found it working for the Five Points Gang in Manhattan. Because he was fairly tall and very strong, Capone was hired to work as a bouncer. He was strong enough to throw out anyone who got too drunk or rowdy at the bar. It was also rumored that he was tough enough to kill two men for the gang, but he was never tried for the murders. Everybody was too scared of the gang to testify against any of its members. They were afraid that if they testified they might be next on the hit list.

The gang bosses liked Capone and gave him a "promotion" to move to Chicago in 1919. By this time, Capone had a wife and an infant son. He set them up in a quiet neighborhood far away from his new office. Then Capone went to work with Johnny Torrio and began to learn the business of being a bootlegger.

The Volstead Act had been passed in 1919, and gangsters already understood that the end of legal liquor sales would be a bonanza for them. Capone set up transportation lines to move alcohol from Canada to Chicago. He met with bootleggers and contracted with them to buy all of the moonshine they could make. Capone would send trucks to pick it up. He purchased warehouses where he could hide and store the illegal liquids and he opened up speakeasies where he could sell it.

> Capone never apologized for the way he made his money. He believed he was providing a "public service" to the people of Chicago.

Soon, Capone was promoted to partner. And when his boss was wounded in an assassination attempt, Capone was tapped to be the new leader of the gang—a gang that was making $100 million dollars a year. Capone was wealthy beyond his wildest dreams.

Capone's Caddy

Al Capone's favorite car was a green and black 1928 Cadillac that he had customized with inch-thick bulletproof glass and armored plating. He had it painted the same colors as the Chicago police cars and equipped it with a police siren and radio. It also had openings in the side and rear window where machine guns could be fired. You can see a video of the car at: http://www.youtube.com/watch?v=qphod_E_AYk

The newspapers loved writing about Al Capone. He dressed in flashy suits of lime and purple. He wore diamond rings, suspenders, and sharp-looking shoes. And he was always willing to talk to the press.

Capone never apologized for the way he made his money. He believed he was providing a "public service" to the people of Chicago. He said, "Ninety percent of the people of Cook County drink and gamble and my offense has been to furnish them with those amusements."

The newspapers took his picture, printed his statements, and covered the stories of his gangland shootouts. And there were lots of shootouts.

Capone ruled the south side of Chicago, but other gangs were always fighting to gain new territory. Because bootlegging was so lucrative, the gangsters had plenty of money. They could afford the newly invented Tommy gun at the outrageous price of $200. (At that time, an automobile cost $400.) Police departments could not afford such expensive weapons, so the gangs had more firepower than most law agencies.

As the head of the south side gang, Capone was not personally involved in the gang shootouts. When there was a killing, like the Valentine's Day massacre, Capone was always out of town—usually out of the state. The police never had evidence that Capone was directly involved in the gang murders, and he was never convicted for any.

The North Side Gang members would have loved to get rid of Al Capone and take over the south side business. In 1926, they made a plan to have Capone killed by spraying his headquarters with machine gun bullets. Capone was unhurt, but 3 weeks later, the leader of the North Side Gang was gunned down. Once again, Capone was out of town and could not be blamed.

With the gang wars going on and the police looking for ways to arrest him, Capone was very careful about his security. He traveled with several bodyguards and assistants.

Al Capone's Florida mansion

When he traveled by train, he would buy out an entire Pullman car. He had his car outfitted with bulletproof glass and reinforced doors. In 1928, he bought a 14-room retreat in Florida, where he could get away and still be guarded.

Capone never registered any property in his own name. He didn't even have a bank account. That way nothing could be traced back to him. It made things very difficult for the police and FBI, who knew that Capone was managing bootleggers, gambling joints, and murders. They were desperate for a way to put Capone behind bars.

It was not the FBI or a police agency that finally sent Al Capone to jail. It was the IRS. After months of research, prosecutors at the IRS found a document from one of Capone's first gambling establishments that had his name on a ledger. It was thin evidence, but the courts used it to their advantage, and in 1932, Al Capone, the notorious gangster, was sent to jail for tax evasion. He was just 33 years old.

After a short stint in an Atlanta prison, Capone was sent to the new federal prison on Alcatraz, an island off the coast of California. Nobody wanted to take a chance on Capone escaping from prison. He spent 7 years in jail and was released in 1939. By that time, Capone's health had failed. After his release, he spent a few weeks in the hospital and then retired to his Florida home. His health continued to decline and he suffered from dementia. Capone died in 1947 after a stroke and a heart attack. He was 48 years old.

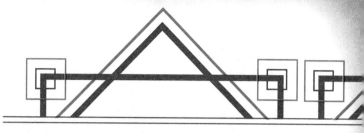

Al Capone's Nicknames

Al Capone hated the nickname Scarface. He disliked the scars on his face and tried to get photographers to take his picture only on his "good" side. His friends called Al "Snorky." It was a Chicago slang term that referred to somebody who dressed in high fashion. Al liked this nickname. He also liked the nicknames "King Alponse" and "Big Fella." But the name he used as an alias was Al Brown.

Al Capone's fully furnished prison cell in an Atlanta prison

THEY CALLED HIM LUCKY

Lucky Luciano, 1936

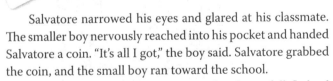

Salvatore narrowed his eyes and glared at his classmate. The smaller boy nervously reached into his pocket and handed Salvatore a coin. "It's all I got," the boy said. Salvatore grabbed the coin, and the small boy ran toward the school.

At 13, Salvatore Lucania was already a full-fledged gangster—making his classmates pay him money so he wouldn't beat them up. Collecting money from other students was the best part of school for Salvatore. He didn't like sitting inside all day and hated his studies. By the time he was 15, he had left school and was running drugs for a New York Mafia boss. He got caught and spent 6 months at a reformatory.

Once he was released, Salvatore immediately returned to his old boss and began working his way up the crime ladder. He was lucky in gambling and got to be an expert at evading arrest. He got so good at it that people started calling him "Lucky." Eventually, he changed his last name to Luciano.

Lucky may not have been a good student, but he was excellent at organization. During Prohibition, Lucky organized and supervised a large bootlegging operation, and by 1925, Lucky Luciano was grossing $12 million a year. In today's money, that would be more than $100 million a year!

He took lessons from his gang boss, Arnold "the Brain" Rothstein, and learned how to navigate high society. He earned the friendship of other gangsters and politicians by giving them tickets to expensive sporting events or donating to politicians' campaigns and charities. He learned how to buy and wear hand-tailored suits and loved expensive handmade leather shoes. He also bribed people with expensive whiskey from Scotland and rum from the Caribbean. By the end of the 1920s, Lucky was one of the top crime bosses in New York City.

Other gang leaders were jealous of Lucky's wealth and power. One day, three men kidnapped Lucky and threw him in the back of a car. They said they were "taking him for a ride." In gangster slang, that meant they were going to take him out into a remote area, beat him up, and kill him. Lucky knew his body would be dumped somewhere back in New York as a warning to his gang members.

The three men did beat Lucky up. They also stabbed him with an ice pick and slit his throat from ear to ear, then dumped his body on a Staten Island beach. Amazingly, Lucky survived the attack. A police officer found his body and sent him to the hospital. Lucky became a legend. He was one of the only gangsters to ever survive "going for a ride."

As soon as Lucky had healed up, he had to face a new problem. From 1930 to 1931, the gangs of New York were fighting it out with each other in an all-out war. Gang members would drive into another gang's territory and machine gun down their enemies. They thought if they killed enough of the other gangs' people, then they could take over. It was a bloody mess, and Lucky Luciano declared it was bad for "business."

Lucky decided to solve the problem. In April of 1931, he lured his own gang's boss, Joe Masseria, to a restaurant on Coney Island. Once he got Joe to the restaurant, four other members of the gang appeared and gunned Joe down. Six months later, he had the rival gang's boss killed. Lucky managed to bring the warring groups together with him as the leader. He called his new group the "Commission." Lucky's commission didn't just unite the warring New York families; it brought together crime families from across the U.S., including Al Capone's outfit.

Genovese helped Luciano gun down Joe Masseria, and later, with Luciano's imprisonment, became acting boss of the Luciano crime family

Vito Genovese, 1934

In 1936, Lucky was arrested and tried for running a prostitution ring. He was sentenced to 30 years in prison and sent to Sing Sing Correctional Facility in Ossining, NY.

Even though he was in jail, Lucky continued to run the operations of the Commission. He sent messages and orders to his men and they obeyed. In 1942, the United States government came to Lucky for help. The government had been suffering from sabotage to ships on the docks of New York. It was so severe

The *Normandie* in New York, 1936

that one luxury liner, the *Normandie*, had blown up. The government knew that Lucky had influence with the New York longshoremen. With a word from Lucky, the sabotage stopped. In gratitude, the U.S. government commuted Lucky's sentence. He was free, with one condition—he was to leave the United States and never come back.

Lucky obeyed. He had been able to run the Commission from behind bars; it would be easier living in Italy. He died of a heart attack in Naples, Italy, in 1962 at the age of 64. More than 300 people attended his funeral, with his body parading through the streets in a horse-drawn carriage. His family received permission to take his body back to New York and bury him in St. John's Cemetery in Queens. Back in New York, more than 2,000 people came to the funeral to say goodbye to Lucky Luciano.

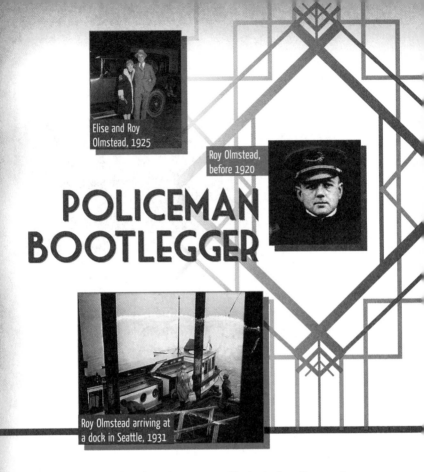

Elise and Roy Olmstead, 1925

Roy Olmstead, before 1920

POLICEMAN BOOTLEGGER

Roy Olmstead arriving at a dock in Seattle, 1931

It was so early that it was still dark by the water. The men were moving fast and silent, lifting crates of liquor from the boat to the cars waiting on the dock. Suddenly, headlights flashed on them and sirens rang out: It was a raid!

The men dropped the boxes and scattered. Roy Olmstead jumped into his waiting car and drove through the bushes and around the police roadblock. He might have gotten away, but he was seen by somebody who knew him—one of his fellow police officers.

Roy Olmstead joined the police force when he was 21 years old and became the youngest lieutenant on the Seattle police force. By 1920, Roy had more than 10 years of experience as a police officer. He had spent time working with the "Dry" squad of Seattle, arresting the rumrunners bringing whiskey and liquor over

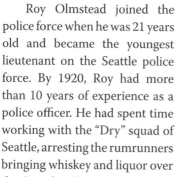

Of course, most of the police were no problem for Roy, because several of them worked for him and most of the businessmen in Seattle bought liquor from him.

the Canadian border. So it was a complete shock to his captain and fellow officers that Roy had taken up a life of crime.

Olmstead surrendered himself to the authorities. He was fired from his job and fined $500. But being fired gave Roy the opportunity to expand his bootleg business. Roy was well-liked and good at organization. He expanded his bootlegging business to hire bookkeepers, drivers, and salesmen. He hired a fleet of vessels, lots of trucks and automobiles, and a staff of mechanics. He became one of Seattle's largest employers, delivering 200 cases of Canadian liquor to the Seattle area every day. Roy even purchased a farm where he would warehouse his illegal liquor away from the prying eyes of the Seattle police.

Of course, most of the police were no problem for Roy, because several of them worked for him and most of the businessmen in Seattle bought liquor from him. Everyone knew Roy Olmstead. They called him the "honest bootlegger," because he never cut his liquor with water and he never allowed his men to carry guns. He told them that none of this was worth anyone's life.

Everyone liked Roy, except for the Prohibition officers for the state of Washington. William Whitney and Roy C. Lyle felt like Olmstead was making fools of them. They became determined to bring him down. They managed to talk one of Roy's men into becoming a spy for them. With information from their spy, Whitney and Lyle wiretapped the phones of Roy's business partners. Eventually they had enough information to get a search warrant and at 2 a.m. on Thanksgiving morning in 1925, the agents arrested Roy Olmsted.

Roy was sentenced to 5 years in jail and had to pay an $8,000 fine. He was released in 1931, and in 1933, Prohibition

Roy's Radio

Radio station KFQX in the Olmstead home in Seattle, 1924

During his bootlegging days, Roy Olmstead was so rich that he and his wife bought one of the first radio stations in Seattle. Roy's wife Elise used to read children's stories on the air. The Feds were sure that she was broadcasting codes to the rumrunners, but they were never able to prove it.

Elise Olmstead reading a story book into a microphone, 1924

was repealed. Roy was never upset about serving time in jail. He said he had broken the law and he had to pay for it. While he was in prison, he began reading the Bible and a book by Christian Scientist Mary Baker Eddy. He became a member of the Christian Science church and in later years was a Sunday school teacher.

Roy spent the next 35 years of his life as a carpenter. He gave up all alcohol and spent time visiting men in prison. When he was asked by people if he was Roy Olmsted, the famous bootlegger, he would respond, "The old Roy Olmstead is dead. He no longer exists."

In 1935, President Franklin D. Roosevelt recognized Roy for his work with the prisoners in King County by granting Roy a full pardon. Roy continued to work with prisoners and the church for the rest of his life. He died in 1966 at the age of 79.

President Franklin D. Roosevelt

QUEEN OF THE BOOTLEGGERS

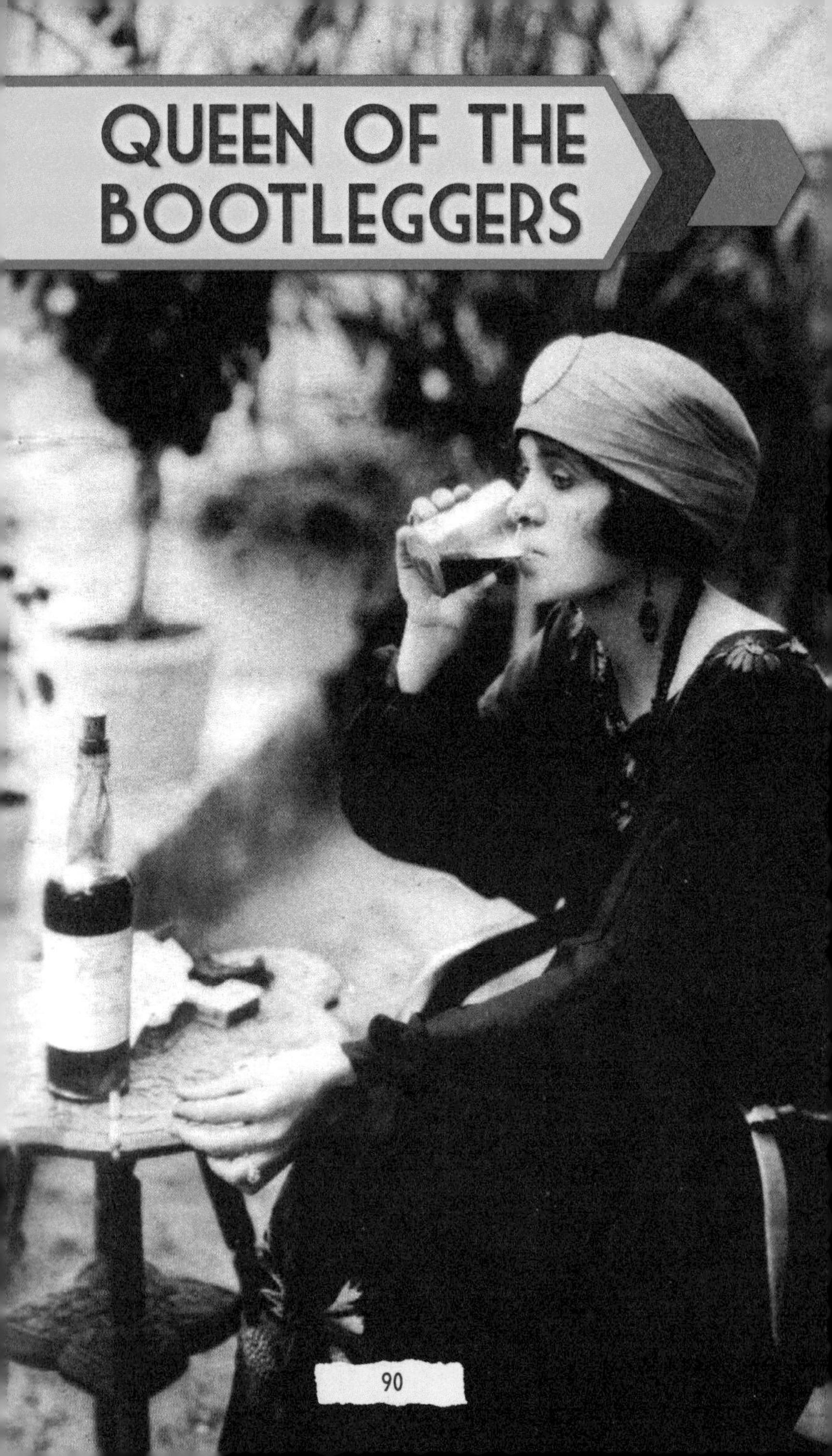

Cleo Lythgoe did not like it when her liquor was insulted. It might be illegal, but it was certainly the highest quality. One day, she heard that a man had been criticizing her liquor, so she tracked him down. He was in the barbershop with his face all lathered up. She marched into the shop and told the man she needed to speak with him. He listened when she said she would blow a hole through him if he ever insulted her merchandise again. Of course, she showed him the gun to prove her point.

Cleo always kept her pistol close at hand. She needed it. She was one of only a handful of women who worked as rumrunners. Men often tried to threaten her, but Cleo stood her ground and kept her pistol loaded.

She was born in Ohio, the 10th child of an English father and Scottish mother. She had dark eyes and olive skin, and looked so exotic that people thought she might be American Indian, Russian, French, or Spanish. At different times, Cleo told people she was from each of those heritages. She told people she had been born in India, that she was a gypsy, and that she was from California. Her story changed whenever she felt like it.

She was not only lovely, she was smart. A British liquor dealer recognized her talents and partnered with her to open up a smuggling operation. They arranged to have liquor legally sent to the Bahamas. From there, Cleo arranged for ships to take the alcohol on into the coast of the United States. The ship contained high-quality Scottish whiskey and European liquors that were in demand from wealthy Americans who were anti-Prohibition.

> Cleo always kept her pistol close at hand. She needed it. She was one of only a handful of women who worked as rumrunners.

Cleo Lythgoe with fellow rumrunner Bill McCoy aboard his alcohol smuggling schooner, the *Tomoka*

The newspaper reporters loved the glamourous Cleo and often asked her for interviews. Cleo thought it was fun to be in the news and was happy to speak to the press, but it brought her some unwelcome attention. Lots of men "fell in love" with Cleo and sent her love letters. Several offered to marry her and save her from her life of crime. In fact, she was so lovely that she earned the nickname Cleo from being compared to Queen Cleopatra (her real name was Gertrude).

Much to their dismay, Cleo repeatedly told them she didn't need a man to tell her what to do.

Strong and independent Cleo took care of herself even when one of her ships was seized and she was arrested. She was charged with smuggling 1,000 cases of whiskey into New Orleans. In reality, she had been somewhere else and she had proof. One of her workers had actually arranged for the drop off and was trying to take the money for himself. Cleo turned him in and was cleared of the charges.

She eventually left the smuggling business and spent time traveling. It was reported that she had stashed away more than a million dollars profit from her rumrunning business. Cleo never admitted to the money, nor did she deny it. But for 25 years, her home was the luxurious Tuller Hotel in Detroit. She lived to be 86 years old.

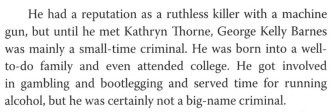

George Kelly Barnes, or Machine Gun Kelly

MACHINE GUN KELLY

He had a reputation as a ruthless killer with a machine gun, but until he met Kathryn Thorne, George Kelly Barnes was mainly a small-time criminal. He was born into a well-to-do family and even attended college. He got involved in gambling and bootlegging and served time for running alcohol, but he was certainly not a big-name criminal.

Then, he met Kathryn and fell hopelessly in love. He married her and was willing to do anything for her—including robbing banks and kidnapping. Kathryn already had a criminal record herself. She had been in and out of jail and knew many of the local crime bosses. Kathryn had been married twice before. Her most recent husband had died of an apparent suicide, but police officers suspected that Kathryn had actually murdered her husband. But there was no good evidence against her, so she could not be charged.

Once Kathryn met George, she decided to "help" him become a better criminal. She bought him a machine gun and urged him to practice. She collected the spent cartridges and would hand them out to patrons of underground drinking clubs. Kathryn said they were "souvenirs" from her husband, "Machine Gun Kelly."

Most historians agree that Kathryn was the inventor of the Machine Gun Kelly image. In reality, George never murdered anyone and only shot his machine gun at bottles and targets. While she was pumping up George's image, Kathryn was also plotting his next job. She was the mastermind behind George's spree of armed bank robberies.

Charles F. Urschel

The next big job Kathryn planned for George was to become a kidnapper. The target was millionaire Oklahoma City oilman, Charles F. Urschel. On a hot night in July, George and his partners walked into Urschel's mansion carrying machine guns. They interrupted a card game and told the Urschels and their guests to be quiet or they'd get their heads blown off.

Two men were playing cards and because the kidnappers didn't know which one was Mr. Urschel, they kidnapped them both. They ordered the two men into the car and took off. Once they were outside of the city, George and his two partners stopped to search for the men's identification. When they figured out which one was Charles Urschel, they let the other man go.

They hid Charles Urschel on a ranch in rural Texas for 8 days. A drop was set up in Kansas City and on July 30, the $200,000 ransom was dropped off at the LaSalle Hotel in Kansas City. It was all in $20 bills with traceable serial numbers, but neither George nor Kathryn knew that.

Charles Urschel was released unhurt. The gangsters divided the ransom money and went their separate ways. George was now known as Machine Gun Kelly in newspapers across the land. Kathryn had done an excellent job in promoting his image. She had done such a good job that Machine Gun Kelly was now on the most wanted list and every law enforcement agency in the country was looking for him.

They found him just a few weeks later, and both George and Kathryn were arrested. George was given a life sentence and spent the rest of his days working in the Alcatraz prison. The whole time, he told everybody that the courts were too hard on his wife. It seems he never fell out of love. He died in prison in 1954.

Kathryn served 25 years in prison and was released in 1958. She went to work as a bookkeeper after she was released.

Kathryn Thorne and Machine Gun Kelly

Alcatraz: "The Rock"

An island just off the coast of San Francisco called Alcatraz became the home to the worst of America's criminals in 1934. It was considered escape-proof because of the barrier of very cold ocean water. There were 36 prisoners who tried to escape. Most of them never made it off the island, but two who did were quickly captured. Five missing inmates have never been accounted for, but it is presumed they drowned during their attempts.

Bonnie Parker and Clyde Barrow, 1933

Some day they'll go down together
And they'll bury them side by side
To few it'll be grief
To the law a relief
But it's death for Bonnie and Clyde

—Written by Bonnie Parker

Bonnie Parker had no illusions of a long life of crime. She and Clyde fully expected to die in a hailstorm of bullets, and they did.

Bonnie Parker was born in Texas in 1910. As a child, she liked reading and writing poetry. She worked hard at her studies and earned honors. Small and pretty, she had dreams of becoming an actress, but in her second year of high school, she met a young man named Roy Thornton and fell madly in love. They were married just a few days before Bonnie turned 16.

Bonnie's new love quickly faded as Thornton was arrested and sent to prison for armed robbery. Bonnie was heartbroken and moved in with her grandmother. But just a year later, Bonnie met a new love. His name was Clyde Barrow.

Clyde had grown up very poor. At one time, his family was so poor that they had to live underneath their wagon until Clyde's mother and father could get enough money to purchase a tent. Clyde did well in school and attended until he was 16. He learned to play both the guitar and the saxophone.

But Clyde's older brother talked him into stealing and learning how to crack safes. Clyde was arrested several times as a teenager, one time for stealing turkeys. He was sent to Eastham Prison Farm in Texas and was severely abused while he was there. In retaliation, he used a lead pipe to smash in the head of the inmate who was abusing him. That was Clyde's first murder. He served 2 years, and when he was released, he declared his goal in life was to get revenge on the Texas prison system for all of the abuse he had suffered while serving time.

In 1932, Clyde and his small gang of followers launched a series of small robberies. Their targets were stores and gas stations, and Clyde's goal was to get enough money so they could buy guns and attack the Eastham prison.

During one of the robberies, Bonnie was arrested and sent to jail. While in jail, Bonnie wrote many poems, including the one that predicted how her life would end. When she was released, Bonnie immediately went back to Clyde.

W. D. Jones and a Rosborough Ford, 1933

The Barrow Gang, as they were called, consisted of Bonnie, Clyde, Buck Barrow, his wife Blanche, Raymond Hamilton, W. D. Jones, and Ralph Fults.

Buck and Blanche Barrow lived with Bonnie and Clyde in a small hideout in Joplin, MO. There, they plotted robberies by day and played cards and drank beer at night. One day, the neighbors were frightened when they heard random gunshots and called the police. When the police arrived, Clyde and Buck opened fire. They killed two policemen and wounded another.

The gang loaded up in their car and sped away, leaving most of their belongings in the house, including a camera and rolls of undeveloped film. When the police processed the film, they found photos of the gang clowning around and posing with guns and cigars. The newspapers printed the photos, and instantly the Barrow Gang became a national headline.

The members of the Barrow gang became celebrities, with their pictures printed everywhere. However, now that they were famous, it became more and more difficult to hide.

The photos fascinated the public. Here were two pretty girls willing to live and work with dangerous criminals. Everyday Americans could not understand this, yet they wanted more stories and more information on the criminals. The members of the Barrow gang became celebrities, with their pictures printed everywhere. However, now that they were famous, it became more and more difficult to hide.

They continued to rob stores and gas stations to make enough money to live on. All the while, Clyde kept planning his revenge on the Texas jail system. On January 16, 1934, Clyde orchestrated the escape of his friend Raymond Hamilton and several other inmates from the Eastham jail. During the escape, the gang shot a prison officer. The Texas Rangers were called in to help hunt down Clyde Barrow and his gang.

Bonnie and Clyde kept on the run for nearly 5 more months. They robbed stores and gas stations all across the South, from Texas through Louisiana. They shot and killed two state troopers and a 60-year-old constable. The public was frightened because of the machine guns they used and their lack of mercy for any of their victims.

The posse that caught Bonnie and Clyde: left to right, standing: Ted Hinton, Prentiss Oakley, and B. M. Gault; sitting: Bob Alcorn, Henderson Jordan, and Frank Hamer

Finally on May 23, 1934, a stakeout in Louisiana proved successful: A posse of lawmen were hidden along a highway, waiting for Bonnie and Clyde's car to come into view. When they identified the vehicle, they let loose with gunfire. In a matter of seconds, both Bonnie and Clyde were dead. Their crime spree had ended, and it had happened just the way Bonnie had predicted more than 2 years earlier.

Their deaths marked the end of the Prohibition gangster era. In the summer of 1934, new federal laws gave the FBI more power and ability to trace criminals. The improvement in two-way radios, police equipment, and cars made it more difficult for the bandit sprees like those carried out by Bonnie and Clyde to continue. By the end of 1934, the FBI had captured or killed other outlaws like John Dillinger, Charles Pretty Boy Floyd, and Baby Face Nelson.

The Lives of Bonnie and Clyde

Want to know more about Bonnie and Clyde? You can watch a short video of their lives at: http://www.biography.com/news/bonnie-and-clyde-9-facts-lifetime-movie-video

QUEENIE

Stephanie St. Clair, or Queenie

She had the most beautiful clothes: stylish gray silk dresses and plush fur coats. She looked like a movie star and lived in a luxurious apartment with a uniformed doorman who called her taxis and monitored her visitors. She was called Queenie or Madame St. Clair and she was the queen of illegal gambling in Harlem in New York City.

Nobody is sure exactly where Stephanie St. Clair was born. She liked to tell people that she came from "European France," and bragged that she spoke flawless European French—not the common French spoken by people of the Caribbean. In reality, she was probably born on either the island of Martinique or Guadeloupe, but she immigrated to America through Marseilles, France.

Once Stephanie hopped off the ship in 1912, she went to work at any job she could find—legal or illegal. In 10 years, she amassed a small fortune—$10,000 in savings. It was the equivalent of $130,000 in today's money. She used the money to set herself up as the "banker" in an illegal lottery.

Queenie's business was so profitable that Dutch Schultz, a White gangster from another part of New York, decided he wanted in on the lottery game.

It was referred to as "the numbers game" or "policy racket." It was played most often in poor neighborhoods of large cities like New York and Chicago. A person would bet that he or she could match three numbers that would be randomly chosen the next day. The gambler would place the bet with a bookie at a speakeasy or some other private establishment. The bet would be recorded on a slip of paper and given to a runner. The runner carried the money and the betting slips to the "bank." Queenie ran the bank. She put up the money against the gamblers' bets and paid out to the winners. She kept the money of the losers. It was very profitable for Queenie.

The people of Harlem saw it as a fun diversion. They bet small amounts and occasionally they won, but the bank was always winning. It is estimated that Queenie earned more than $200,000 per year with her bank. That would be the same as $2 million a year in today's money. She could afford all of the dresses, fur coats, and fancy apartments she wanted.

There was just one problem. The lottery system was totally illegal. The police were supposed to arrest gamblers and their bookies. But Queenie employed a lot of people as bookies and runners. She also donated to charities in Harlem and invested in legitimate businesses. The people of Harlem were angry when the police would harass her. And Queenie also paid many of the officers money so they would "ignore" her business.

Queenie's business was so profitable that Dutch Schultz, a White gangster from another part of New York, decided he wanted in on the lottery game. Queenie was not pleased. It is said that she cussed Dutch out in English, French, and Spanish. She also engaged in a shooting war with him. Her bodyguards and workers were shot at by Dutch's men and several of them were killed. Queenie retaliated and the war raged on with other gangsters' groups joining in. In the end, more than 40 people were killed

In the midst of the war, Lucky Luciano's group attacked Dutch and he was mortally wounded. Queenie denied that she had anything to do with his shooting, but she did send a telegram to the hospital where he lay dying. The telegram said, "As ye sow, so shall ye reap." She signed it Madame Queen.

There are more stories about Queenie, but many of them cannot be verified. It is believed that she married a Harlem activist named Sufi Abdul Hamid and that she shot him when she caught him cheating on her. Queenie said the gun went off accidentally. Hamid survived, but the marriage didn't.

Queenie was convicted of first-degree assault and possession of a concealed weapon. She served a short sentence in prison. When she was released, she returned to Harlem and lived out the rest of her life in her elegant apartment with plenty of clothes and money to last until her death at the age of 73.

GET THE GOODS

Balloon-Powered Boat

Rumrunner schooner *Kirk and Sweeney* with contraband stacked on deck

Rumrunners always wanted to have the fastest boat possible so they could outrun the Coast Guard. Of course, the Coast Guard also wanted to have the fastest and best boats, too. It was a contest to see who could build a better boat.

You can build your own boat and race it in the tub or pool.

Materials

- Floating container such as a Styrofoam plate, milk carton, butter container, etc.
- Plastic bendy straw
- Rubber band
- Balloon
- Putty or clay

Poke a hole in one side of your floating container. Make the hole the same size as the drinking straw. Then, attach the balloon to the nonbendy end of the straw with the rubber band. Be careful to keep from smashing the straw. Poke the bendy end of the straw through the hole in the container. If necessary, plug the space around the straw with clay to keep it from leaking. Blow up the balloon through the straw and put your finger over the tip of the straw. Put the straw under water and take your finger off the tip. Watch your boat move!

GET THE GOODS

Wanted Poster

Make your own Most Wanted Poster just like those federal agents used to track down gangsters and criminals. You may be able to catch a neighborhood criminal mastermind or the sister who ate your favorite snack!

John Dillingers wanted poster, 1934

WANTED
DEAD OR ALIVE

Reward: $10,000

BIBLIOGRAPHY

AUTHOR'S NOTE

Dear Readers,

I hope you liked learning the truth in the *Top Secret Files*. I have worked hard to research each story and verify its authenticity. Sometimes there are differences of opinions between historians as to what exactly happened and when. I've used the information that is currently regarded as true. But like every good mystery, sometimes new clues will be found and this might change our view of history.

The quotes in these books are words that the historical figures used. I have tried to capture the spirit of when and how the words would have been heard; therefore, sometimes the dialogue has been embellished or re-imagined to fit the spirit of the story. As a history detective, I will continue to research and dig for clues that will tell me more about history and the people who made it. You might want to look into some of the sources I used for my research (listed below) if you are interested in learning more about this fascinating period of history.

—Stephanie Bearce

BOOKS

Behr, E. (2011). *Prohibition: Thirteen years that changed America.* New York, NY: Arcade Publishing.

Buhk, T. (2014). *True Crime: Michigan: The state's most notorious cases.* Mechanicsburg, PA: Stackpole Books.

Burrough, B. (2004). *Public enemies: America's greatest crime wave and the birth of the FBI, 1933–34.* New York, NY: Penguin.

Hoffman, D. E. (1993). *Scarface Al and the crime crusaders: Chicago's private war against Capone.* Carbondale and Edwardsville: Southern Illinois University Press.

Eig, J. (2010). *Get Capone: The secret plot that captured America's most wanted gangster.* New York, NY: Simon and Schuster.

Kobler, J. (1995). *Ardent spirits: The rise and fall of Prohibition.* New York, NY: G.P. Putnams's Sons.

Mappen, M. (2013). *Prohibition gangsters: The rise and fall of a bad generation.* New Brunswick, NJ: Rutgers University Press.

Ness, E., & Fraley, O. (1976). *The untouchables.* New York, NY: American Reprint Company.

Okrent, D. (2010). *Last call: The rise and fall of Prohibition.* New York, NY: Scribner.

Peck, G. (2011). *Prohibition in Washington, D.C.: How dry we weren't.* Mount Pleasant, SC: The History Press.

Pegram, T. P. (1998). *Battling demon rum: The struggle for a Dry America, 1800–1933.* Chicago, IL: Ivan R. Dee.

WEBSITES

1920's Fashion and Music. (n.d.). *4 famous flappers of the 1920s.* Retrieved from http://www.1920s-fashion-and-music.com/flappers-of-the-1920s.html

Abbott, K. (2012). Prohibition's premier hooch hounds. *Smithsonian Magazine.* Retrieved from http://www.smith sonianmag.com/history/prohibitions-premier-hooch-hounds-16963599/?no-ist

Alcatraz Facts and Figures. (n.d.). *Alcatraz—Quick facts.* Retrieved from http://www.alcatrazhistory.com/factsnfig. htm

Alcatraz History.com. (n.d.). *Machine Gun Kelly.* Retrieved from http://www.alcatrazhistory.com/mgk.htm

Balloon powered boat. (2011). Retrieved from http://alittle learningfortwo.blogspot.com/2011/05/balloon-power ed-boat.html

Biography.com. (n.d.). *Al Capone.* Retrieved from http://www. biography.com/people/al-capone-9237536

Biography.com. (n.d.). *Lucky Luciano.* Retrieved from http://www.biography.com/people/lucky-luciano-9388 350#early-life

Bonnie and Clyde. (n.d.). Retrieved from http://en.wikipedia. org/wiki/Bonnie_and_Clyde

Bragg, M. (2012). Meet Congress' favorite bootlegger: Prohibition, hypocrisy, and "the man in the green hat." *Reason.com.* Retrieved from http://reason.com/reasontv/ 2012/12/05/the-true-story-of-congress-bootlegger-pr

Bureau of Prohibition. (n.d.). Retrieved from http://en. wikipedia.org/wiki/Bureau_of_Prohibition

Clara Bow. (n.d.). Retrieved from https://en.wikipedia.org/ wiki/Clara_Bow

Colvin, D., & Kehl, T. (n.d.). *1920's bootlegging: How it was enforced.* Retrieved from http://1920sbootlegging.weebly. com/how-it-was-enforced.html

Dickens, D. (2012). Ruthless gun molls behind the Mob's infamous gangsters. *BuzzFeed.* Retrieved from http://www. buzzfeed.com/donnad/ruthless-gun-molls-behind-the-mobs-infamous-gangs#.xvLaxMom2

Drink Michigan. (2013). *Prohibition in Michigan.* Retrieved from http://www.drinkmichigan.org/prohibition-michigan/

Elizebeth Friedman. (n.d.). Retrieved from http://en.wikipedia.org/wiki/Elizebeth_Friedman

Federal Bureau of Investigation. (n.d.). *Kansas City massacre—Charles Arthur "Pretty Boy" Floyd.* Retrieved from http://www.fbi.gov/about-us/history/famous-cases/kansas-city-massacre-pretty-boy-floyd

Flynn, C. (2014). *15 fascinating facts about Al Capone.* Retrieved from http://www.yurtopic.com/society/people/al-capone-facts.html

Foulsen, E. (n.d.). *Evelyn Frechette: I give my love.* Retrieved from http://dillingerswomen.com/molls/billie.html

Frank McErlane. (n.d.). Retrieved from https://en.wikipedia.org/wiki/Frank_McErlane

Galindo, B. (2013). 15 surprising facts about Prohibition. *BuzzFeed.* Retrieved from http://www.buzzfeed.com/briangalindo/15-surprising-facts-about-prohibition#.nmv8a5VD2

George Cassiday. (n.d.). Retrieved from https://en.wikipedia.org/wiki/George_Cassiday

Houston, R. (2012). *NASCAR's earliest days forever connected to bootlegging.* Retrieved from http://www.nascar.com/en_us/news-media/articles/2012/11/01/moonshine-mystique.html

Huff, D. (n.d.). *Twenties slang.* Retrieved from http://www.huffenglish.com/gatsby/slang.html

Jamie named to aid 'Secret Six' in crime drive. (1930, October 31). *Chicago Daily Tribune.* Retrieved from http://archives.chicagotribune.com/1930/10/31/page/3/article/jamie-named-to-aid-secret-six-in-crime-drive

John, F. D. J. (2012). *"Oregon's outback" was real moonshiner's paradise in '20s.* Retrieved from http://www.offbeatoregon.com/1203c-moonshiners-of-oregon-outback.html

Library of Congress. (2013). *Topics in chronicling America: Carrie Nation, "saloon smasher" and temperance lecturer.* Retrieved from http://www.loc.gov/rr/news/topics/carrie nation.html

Ling, S. J. (2011). *Gertrude Lythgoe—Fascinating women of Prohibition.* Retrieved from http://sallyjling.org/2011/06/28/gertrude-lythgoe-fascinating-women-of-prohibi tion

Lucky Luciano. (n.d.). Retrieved from http://en.wikipedia.org/wiki/Lucky_Luciano

Maeder, J. (1998, April 22). Rumhounds Izzy and Moe, 1925. *New York Daily News.* Retrieved from http://www.ny dailynews.com/archives/news/rumhounds-izzy-moe-1925-article-1.787185

McClary, D. C. (2002). *Olmstead, Roy (1886–1966)—King of King County bootleggers.* Retrieved from http://www.historylink.org/index.cfm?DisplayPage=output.cfm&File _Id=4015

Miley, M. (2011). *Gimme some hooch!* Retrieved from https://marymiley.wordpress.com/tag/prohibition-slang

Minnick, F. (2014). Women's History Month spotlight: Women bootleggers. *Huffington Post.* Retrieved from http://www.huffingtonpost.com/fred-minnick/womens-history-month-spot_b_4927284.html

The Outlaw Journals. (n.d.). *Like tainted meat: Detroit's 'Kosher Nostra.'* Retrieved from http://www.babyfacenelson journal.com/purple-gang.html

The Outlaw Journals. (n.d.). *The trail grows cold.* Retrieved from http://www.babyfacenelsonjournal.com/kansas-city-massacre-2.html

The Purple Gang. (n.d.). Retrieved from http://en.wikipedia.org/wiki/The_Purple_Gang

Quotes by and about Capone. (2006). Retrieved from http://www.mistercapone.com/quotes.htm

Sismondo, C. (2013). *Bathtub gin, blind tigers, and bootleggers: The language of the speakeasy.* Retrieved from http://blog.oxforddictionaries.com/2013/01/speakeasy

Sneaky smugglers. (n.d.). *Walkerville Times Magazine.* Retrieved from http://www.walkervilletimes.com/34/sneaky-smugglers.html

Sroka, S. L. (2011). Revisionist history: The historical reality of Eliot Ness and the Untouchables. *Chicago Tribune.* Retrieved from http://articles.chicagotribune.com/2011-10-16/opinion/ct-perspec-1016-untouchables-20111016_1_al-capone-eliot-ness-elmer-irey/2

State Historical Society of Missouri. (n.d.). *Carry A. Nation (1846–1911).* Retrieved from http://shs.umsystem.edu/historicmissourians/name/n/nation/

United States Senate. (n.d.). *February 18, 1930: The man in the green hat.* Retrieved from http://www.senate.gov/artandhistory/history/minute/The_Man_in_the_Green_Hat.htm

Waugh, C. (2015). 20 mind-blowing facts about Al Capone. *What Culture.* Retrieved from http://whatculture.com/history/20-mind-blowing-facts-about-al-capone.php/9

Weiser, K. (2014). *Speakeasies of the Prohibition era.* Retrieved from http://www.legendsofamerica.com/ah-prohibitionspeakeasy2.html

Wilson, B. (2013). *Bootlegging and NASCAR: From moonshining to racing.* Retrieved from http://news.boldride.com/2013/12/bootlegging-and-nascar-from-moonshining-to-racing/41671/

Woodward, M. (n.d.). *Roy Olmstead: Seattle's "Rum King."* Retrieved from http://www.rainiervalleyhistory.org/stories/articles/roy-olmstead-seattles-rum-king

YourDictionary. (n.d.). *20s gangster slang.* Retrieved from http://grammar.yourdictionary.com/slang/20s-gangster-slang.html

ABOUT THE
AUTHOR

Stephanie Bearce is a writer, a teacher, and a history detective. She loves tracking down spies and uncovering secret missions from the comfort of her library in St. Charles, MO. When she isn't writing or teaching, Stephanie loves to travel the world and go on adventures with her husband, Darrell.

Stealthy spies, secret weapons, and special missions are just part of the mysteries uncovered when kids dare to take a peek at the *Top Secret Files*. Featuring books that focus on often unknown aspects of history, this series is sure to hook even the most reluctant readers, taking them on a journey as they try to unlock some of the secrets of our past.

Top Secret Files: The American Revolution

George Washington had his own secret agents, hired pirates to fight the British, and helped Congress smuggle weapons, but you won't learn that in your history books! Learn the true stories of the American Revolution and how spies used musket balls, books, and laundry to send messages. Discover the female Paul Revere, solve a spy puzzle, and make your own disappearing ink. It's all part of the true stories from the *Top Secret Files: The American Revolution*.

ISBN-13: 978-1-61821-247-4

Top Secret Files: The Civil War

The Pigpen Cipher, the Devil's Coffee Mill, and germ warfare were all a part of the Civil War, but you won't learn that in your history books! Discover the truth about Widow Greenhow's spy ring, how soldiers stole a locomotive, and the identity of the mysterious "Gray Ghost." Then learn how to build a model submarine and send secret light signals to your friends. It's all part of the true stories from the *Top Secret Files: The Civil War*.

ISBN-13: 978-1-61821-250-4

Top Secret Files: The Cold War

Poison dart umbrellas, lipstick pistols, and cyanide guns were all a part of the arsenal of tools used by spies of the Soviet KGB, American CIA, and British MI6, but you won't learn that in your history books! Discover how East Germans tried to ride zip lines to freedom, while the Cambridge Four infiltrated Britain and master spy catchers like Charles Elwell were celebrated. Then make your own secret codes and practice sending shoe messages. It's all part of the true stories from the *Top Secret Files: The Cold War*.

ISBN-13: 978-1-61821-419-5 • **Available August 2015**

Top Secret Files: Pirates and Buried Treasure

Pirates of the Golden Age had to deal with scurvy, fight ferocious battles, and eat everything from monkeys to snakes to sea turtles, but you won't learn that in your history books! Discover the truth about Anne Bonny, the Irish woman who was a true Pirate of the Caribbean, and the secrets of Blackbeard and the daring pirate Cheng I Sao. Then learn how to talk like a pirate and make a buried treasure map for your friends. It's all part of the true stories from the *Top Secret Files: Pirates and Buried Treasure*.

ISBN-13: 978-1-61821-421-8 • **Available August 2015**

Top Secret Files: The Wild West

Bandits, lawmen, six shooters, bank robberies, and cowboys were all a part of the Wild West. But so were camels, buried treasure, and gun-slinging dentists. Dive into strange tales like the mysterious Cave of Gold, filled with ancient skeletons, and Rattle Snake Dick's lost fortune. Discover the truth about notorious legends like Jesse James, Buffalo Bill, former spy-turned-bandit Belle Star, and Butch Cassidy and the Sundance Kid. Then, learn why it's unlucky to have a dead man's hand when playing cards and how to talk like a real cowpoke. It's all part of the true stories from the *Top Secret Files: The Wild West*.

ISBN-13: 978-1-61821-462-1 • **Available October 2015**

Top Secret Files: World War I

Flame throwers, spy trees, bird bombs, and Hell Fighters were all a part of World War I, but you won't learn that in your history books! Uncover long-lost secrets of spies like Howard Burnham, "The One Legged Wonder," and nurse-turned-spy, Edith Cavell. Peek into secret files to learn the truth about the Red Baron and the mysterious Mata Hari. Then learn how to build your own Zeppelin balloon and mix up some invisible ink. It's all part of the true stories from the *Top Secret Files: World War I*.

ISBN-13: 978-1-61821-241-2

Top Secret Files: World War II

Spy school, poison pens, exploding muffins, and Night Witches were all a part of World War II, but you won't learn that in your history books! Crack open secret files and read about the mysterious Ghost Army, rat bombs, and doodlebugs. Discover famous spies like the White Mouse, super-agent Garbo, and baseball player and spy, Moe Berg. Then build your own secret agent kit and create a spy code. It's all part of the true stories from the *Top Secret Files: World War II*.

ISBN-13: 978-1-61821-244-3